ALABAMA
SCOUNDRELS

ALABAMA SCOUNDRELS

OUTLAWS, PIRATES, BANDITS & BUSHWHACKERS

KELLY KAZEK & WIL ELRICK

THE
History
PRESS

Published by The History Press
Charleston, SC 29403
www.historypress.net

First published 2014

ISBN 978.1.5402.1041.8

Library of Congress Cataloging-in-Publication Data

Kazek, Kelly.
Alabama scoundrels : outlaws, pirates, bandits & bushwhackers / Kelly Kazek and William
Elrick.
pages cm. -- (True crime)
ISBN 978-1-62619-533-2 (paperback)
1. Criminals--Alabama--History. 2. Outlaws--Alabama--History. 3. Crime--Alabama--
History. I. Title.
HV6793.A2K39 2014
364.1092'2761--dc23
2014018003

To the adventures that have brought me to this point in life and, more so, to the adventures that will take me into tomorrow.
—Wil Elrick

To my kids—Shannon, Zane and Ezra.
—Kelly Kazek

CONTENTS

INTRODUCTION

W hen you hear the word *outlaw*, most of the time, your mind will jump to the Wild West of the late 1800s plains—the men with bandanas pulled over their faces robbing a stagecoach or hijacking a train, the brazen bank robberies that took place in newly settled towns and the high-noon showdown between the outlaw gunman and the local sheriff. But these images from television, movies and books only show the surface of the outlaw existence.

In the first half century of our country's existence, Alabama was considered the Wild West as settlers embraced Manifest Destiny and moved farther from the East Coast and our founding settlements. The land was harsh, the settlements were scattered and people had to be tough to survive. It was a perfect setting for lawlessness.

The people who began settling the state in the early 1800s were hardy, resourceful and fearless. The only law most settlers lived by was that of the land, and it was every family for itself until settlers began to gather in communities.

With statehood in 1819 came more people, laws, businesses, towns and, of course, trouble. With each community came men who wanted to steal or cause destruction. We call these men outlaws, scoundrels, bushwhackers or any number of colorful names, but one thing remains constant: they used violence to accomplish their goals.

As communities formed, more laws were created, and peace officers were needed to enforce them. Oftentimes, those charged with enforcing the governmental laws walked a thin line between criminal and lawman. It was not unusual for a man considered an outlaw in one community to be found as a sheriff or constable in another.

Alabama Scoundrels: Outlaws, Pirates, Bandits & Bushwhackers brings to life more than two dozen of the most infamous lawbreakers to set foot on Alabama soil. The lives of these men span our history starting in the early eighteenth century when pirates sailed our coastal waters, followed by the nineteenth century when law and order began to rule the day and ending in the twentieth century when the Industrial Revolution helped develop a more orderly society.

The crimes these scoundrels were accused of committing vary as widely as the personalities of the men themselves. You will find tales of the pirate Jean Lafitte, Civil War–era bushwhackers Colonel Joseph Sanders and Milus Johnston, Lincoln assassination conspirator Lewis Powell, social activist turned anarchist Albert Parsons, one-time vice president Aaron Burr, cult leader turned murderer "Bloody" Bob Sims and the mysterious hobo outlaw Railroad Bill.

From their starts to their finishes, the lives of well-known gunslingers with ties to the state are also described on these pages, including John Wesley Hardin, outlaw Tom Clark, Rube Burrow, James Copeland, outlaw sheriff Steve Renfroe, Bart Thrasher and two of the most widely known outlaws in our nation's history, Frank and Jesse James.

WHAT MAKES AN OUTLAW?

The term *outlaw* dates as far back as ancient Rome as a legal concept. The word meant "outside the protection of the law," which, in effect, gave permission for vigilante justice. In ancient times, citizens were legally empowered to kill anyone who was designated an outlaw. In the early days of settling Alabama, vigilante justice was not legally recognized, although it was often given taciturn approval.

Historians list numerous factors that made the nineteenth century the perfect time for breeding outlaws, including sparse populations with easy hiding places, fewer banks so that citizens carried their valuables with them when they traveled and the harsh realities of a time when people were struggling merely to survive. Upheaval from the Civil War and Reconstruction also bred many outlaws.

In the newly formed territories and states, tracking criminals across vast and wild lands was treacherous and time consuming. Some of the outlaws in this book managed to outsmart justice, disappearing into history with their dates and places of death unknown, but many more faced violent ends, often at the end of a hangman's noose or a gun barrel.

Becoming Alabama

Famed Spanish explorer Hernando De Soto initially entered what would become Alabama in 1539, but it would be more than 160 years before the area was settled.

In the eighteenth century, coastal areas of the state were popular sites for settling because of the reliance on sea travel. Dauphin Island, initially known as Massacre Island, was settled by French explorer Pierre Le Moyne d'Iberville in 1699, while other areas that now make up Baldwin and Mobile Counties were part of Spanish West Florida in 1783, the Republic of West Florida in 1810 and the Mississippi Territory in 1812.

Much of what is now northern Alabama was initially considered part of the Yazoo lands and then, after 1767, was under the province of Georgia during colonization by the British through the Revolutionary War. The lower third of Alabama became part of the Mississippi Territory in 1798, with the Yazoo lands added to the territory in 1804.

Before Mississippi was admitted to the United States of America in 1817, the eastern portion of the Mississippi Territory was split off and named the Alabama Territory. St. Stephens, now defunct, was Alabama's territorial capital. The Alabama Territory was granted statehood in 1819.

Later that year, the U.S. Congress selected Huntsville as the site of the state's first Constitutional Convention, and the north Alabama city served as the temporary capital of Alabama until 1820.

Capitals in Alabama were:

- Huntsville in Madison County, 1819–20
- Cahaba in Dallas County (now a ghost town), 1820–25
- Tuscaloosa in Tuscaloosa County, 1826–46
- Montgomery in Montgomery County, 1847–present

The first capital building in Montgomery was built in 1847 but burned in 1849. It was replaced with the existing building in 1851.

During this time when legislators were organizing the state of Alabama and writing its laws, some of its citizens were doing their best to break them and escape the state's justice.

CHAPTER 1

BLOODY BOB SIMS

A "PROPHET" AND THE CHOCTAW COUNTY WAR

It was Christmas Day 1891, and more than five hundred people had gathered from across southeast Alabama determined to see the end, once and for all, of Bob Sims, his lawless "church" and his bloody ways. Those who weren't there to physically force Sims to justice were there to witness it. It was the most excitement seen in Choctaw County's history.

The posse surrounded the Sims home, cornering Sims, his wife, their children and several church members, known as Simsites. The local sheriff led the mob and sent orders for someone to go fetch the old Civil War cannon from Bladon Springs to blast Sims out.

"Sims!" someone hollered. "We're bringing in the cannon."

The weapon was taking too long to arrive, so a few of the men reportedly cut down a tree and blackened the trunk in an effort to spook Sims. It worked. Soon, Robert Sims shouted from the house and made an offer. He'd give himself up if Sheriff Gavin would promise to protect him and his followers from the angry mob.

Robert Sims, known as "Bloody Bob Sims," formed a church with followers known as "Simsites." *Encyclopedia of Alabama.*

The sheriff agreed he'd do what he could and took Sims, Tom Savage and Tom's nephews—Will and Tyree Savage—into custody. Sims's wife and daughters also were arrested.

Finally, Bloody Bob Sims was in custody. But would townspeople be satisfied with that?

ROBERT BRUCE SIMS was born in Bladen County, North Carolina, in 1839. He married a woman named Eliza, and they started a 240-acre farm in Choctaw County, Alabama. They raised two sons, Lacheus Bailey and Epaminondas, and four daughters, Laura, Clara, Ruby and Elisabeth.

Outwardly, Bob Sims was an unlikely outlaw. A Confederate veteran who fought with the Twenty-second Alabama Infantry, Sims was injured and captured by Union troops and imprisoned at Camp Morton in Indiana.

Following his harrowing experiences in the Civil War, Sims resumed farming in the Womack Hill community of Choctaw County and, at one time, served as county road surveyor. For a time, he lived peacefully among his neighbors, but a series of court cases changed his outlook toward authority. In one case, after threatening his brother-in-law, Sims was found guilty of using insulting language and fined twenty dollars.

He grew angry with the court system and its insistence on having him swear an oath, which he said violated the laws of God. In one court case in which Sims was involved, he referred to Judge Luther Smith as "Satan."

The family attended the local Methodist church, but as Sims's beliefs grew more divergent from standard teachings, he became at odds with local pastors. For instance, on one occasion, Sims reportedly attended a church revival at which the pastor asked members to kneel at the altar. Sims refused, saying it was against his beliefs to bow to anyone but God.

In 1877, he purportedly was attending Womack Hill Methodist Church until one Sunday, he suddenly proclaimed the church was abusing the Gospel and caused such a scene that he was convicted of disturbing a church service, a crime at the time, and fined seventy-five dollars.

Unhappy with any denomination, Sims began his own church and preached a strict adherence to the Old Testament and observed Sabbath on Saturdays. According to legend, his ability to remember and quote biblical passages was nothing short of astonishing. Eventually, he amassed more than one hundred followers, including his family. He began publishing a pamphlet called *The Veil Is Rent*, which became his church's doctrine. In one article, Sims calls for the destruction of civil authority because it was the devil's work.

The trouble for the Simsites began when Bob Sims started a moonshine business. Believing God's was the only true law, Sims did not follow man's laws and believed he did not have to pay taxes on land, goods or his liquor.

Not only did pastors of other local churches disapprove of his teachings, but they also felt liquor was the devil's work and loudly preached against its evils at every opportunity.

The fighting began in 1891, when one of Sims's followers wanted to court the daughter of Reverend Richard Bryant Carroll, a pastor from Soulwipa who preached against Sims's moonshining. On May 1, Carroll turned up dead.

Carroll allegedly sent his daughter's suitor away, and someone returned that night and shot Carroll dead on his porch. Although no one was arrested, members of the community suspected Sims and his followers.

The Reverend Carroll, now listed as the first fatality of the Sims war, was buried in Harrison Cemetery as townspeople began to wonder how to handle the growing problem of Bob Sims and his religious sect. Several people reported Sims to federal authorities in Mobile for moonshining. One of those citizens was local store owner John McMillan, whose fate would become entwined with Sims's before the year was over.

By this time, area newspapers had begun reporting the goings-on in Choctaw County, calling Sims's church a "sect" whose members believed Sims was their prophet.

On May 28, 1891, the *Hamilton Times* in Marion County reported another incident in which a Sims follower refused to follow government rule. The newspaper reported:

> One of this sect was called to serve on the jury in the United States court here today [May 25]. He refused to take an oath, because of the biblical prohibition and was permitted to affirm. Then he announced that he would never convict any one, because the Bible says "judge not." Inquiry shows that the brother of this juror, a man named Robert Simms [sic], runs an illicit distillery in Choctaw County, and when the deputy marshal served a warrant on him last week, Simms [sic] tore the document to pieces, saying that he was under no man's authority. His brother says there is no concealment in the case. Simms [sic] claims that he has the right to do as he pleases and that any attempt to stop his distillery will be religious persecution.

That summer, the federal marshal and his men made several attempts to capture the moonshiners, but during each raid, the federals were outnumbered. Finally, in late summer, the federals caught Sims unaware and

A SOUTHERN TERROR.

Arrest of the Bloody Bob Sims and
His Bad Gang.

IT MAY BE A CASE FOR LYNCH.

A Dramatic Repetition of One of the
Worst Outrages Ever Perpetrated in
any Country, Civilized or Savage,
Christian or Heathen.

This clipping from an 1891
story in the *Pittsburgh Press
Gazette* shows public sentiment
against Bloody Bob Sims.
Public domain.

were able to take him into custody and ride to Bladon Springs to await a steamboat to transfer Sims to jail in Mobile.

While the men were given lodging in a local hotel, Sims was placed under guard in an outbuilding. Late that night, Sims's brothers Jim and Neal and his son Bailey Sims rode into town along with three Simsites. They managed to break Bob Sims from his jail, but in the ensuing gunfight, Bailey Sims was killed, along with a bystander, Dr. A.B. Pugh. Jim Sims was injured and captured.

Townspeople grew nervous of Sims's retribution for the death of his son and capture of his brother. The federal marshals stayed on to help protect the public. But soon, nerves turned to outrage, and residents, tired of the Simsites' bloody ways, retrieved Jim from his makeshift cell two days after Sims's escape and hanged him from a nearby tree.

The bodies of Bailey and Jim eventually were retrieved by some of Bob's children, and the men were buried in the Sims family cemetery behind the Simses' house.

The federals, ill equipped to deal with the Sims clan, returned to Mobile with the intent to return with more supplies and men. But the townspeople were growing impatient with the federals' approach and wanted the Simses stopped.

A posse of local residents formed and rode out to the Simses' house in search of Bob and Neal. The men were not at the homestead, so members of the posse issued a warning: get out of Choctaw County or else. A few family members who feared for their lives, including two of Sims's daughters, left to live with family in Mississippi.

All through that fall, Bob and Neal managed to remain in hiding. Sims's daughters who had taken refuge in Mississippi returned home, purportedly with a promise from the governor that they would remain unmolested.

In Sims's absence, yet another lawsuit was filed in Choctaw County court, and the Sims homestead was put up for auction to pay a settlement ordered by the judge. The news drew Sims from hiding, and he returned to prevent his home from being sold. In the meantime, Sims was also nursing a grudge against local businessman John McMillan, who owned a store in Paragon. Rumors had flown that McMillan was the first to turn in Sims to federal agents, and Sims wanted revenge. But his vengeful act would be the last straw for residents.

On December 22, 1891, Sims and his henchman Will Savage waited at the crossroads near Gilbertown and hijacked a wagon hauling merchandise to McMillan's store. After the merchandise was unloaded, Sims gave the driver a message: "Tell McMillan we're coming for him, and we're going to burn his house down." The driver duly warned McMillan, who gathered a group of men to stand guard on his property that night. When nothing happened, McMillan assumed Sims's threat was idle and made the fatal decision to call off the guards.

Newspapers of the time gave numerous accounts of what happened next, but most agree that Sims and some of his followers surrounded McMillan's home just past bedtime on December 23 and set it ablaze. Those living inside—including women and ten children—awoke to the smell of smoke and, one by one, ran from the burning home. As they exited the home, Sims and his followers opened fire, indiscriminately killing anyone who ran out. When the shooting stopped, one adult and three children were dead. At least nine others, including Belle McKenzie, a young teacher boarding at the home, were wounded. Belle died from her wounds three weeks later.

This series of events led to the Christmas Eve siege of the Sims home, which, by that point, was fortified with weapons and supplies. The citizens, with little patience left for Sims's violent ways, were ready to take matters into their own hands and had already found and lynched Bob's brother John Sims that same night. The local sheriff was doing his best to orchestrate a surrender. The angry mob waited throughout Christmas Eve and into Christmas Day for Sims to come out of his homestead. Several barrages of gunfire were exchanged until finally, under threat of cannon fire, Sims gave up late Christmas Day.

On December 27, 1891, the *New York Times* reported, "When Sims heard of this preparation to blow his stronghold to splinters he looked at his women folk and his heart misgave him. He began a parley with the Sheriff at 2 o'clock, he said he would surrender if the posse would do him no injury and if the posse would protect him from mob violence."

The men discussed the proposition for two hours, the newspaper account said: "At first the proposal of Sims was flatly refused but the fact that there were women in the house was a strong point in favor of mercy for the inmates. The thought of shooting with a cannon into a house harboring women was so repugnant that it overcame the almost wild longing for the blood of the men outlaws so that at last the terms of Sims were accepted."

The sheriff took Sims into custody, as well as Tom, Will and Tyree Savage, promising Sims he would do what he could to keep the angry mob at bay.

Several news accounts report that Sims's wife and daughters, dressed in men's clothing, had taken part in murders at the McMillan homestead, an account that has never been proven. However, newspapers, including the *New York Times*, reported four women were taken into custody along with Sims and the Savages to be transported to jail at Butler.

Escorted by a posse of twenty-five men for protection, two wagons headed for the jail, one carrying the men and another the women. Soon, the angry mob caught up to the wagons, and the four men were jerked from inside and strung up on nearby trees.

The *Times* reported: "Bob was asked if he had anything to say. He replied: 'Take my hand, feel my pulse and see if I'm a coward.'"

Within minutes, the four men were dead. The women, however, were spared.

The *New York Times* reported on December 29, 1891, that casualties were still being tallied in the Sims war. The newspaper account reported that in addition to the four men hanged on Christmas Day and John Sims, who was hanged on Christmas Eve, townspeople had hanged Bob's nephew Mosely Sims and were in pursuit of another follower who reportedly took part in the McMillan family massacre. The *Times* reported:

> The most alarming thing about the situation is that *Neal Sims*, the brother of *Bob*, and who rescued Bob from the Deputy Marshal at Slandon Springs [sic], in Choctaw county, Aug. 20 last, is still at large and is determined to avenge Bob's death. Neal is a desperate man. He firmly believes that his brother was a prophet from God and had divine sanction to kill off the devil's agents—namely the officers of the law. Neal Sims has collected nearly forty of the Simsites and sent word Sunday that he intended to assault and burn the village of Womac Hill before the night of that day. The people were greatly excited and all of Sunday were massing at Womac Hill to defend the place.
>
> The enraged people on Saturday morning after the lynching of Bob Sims and his four followers, wrecked Sims' house, and burned it to the ground, then killed every living thing on the place except the members of the family, who escaped to a neighbor's house, and who will move as soon as possible to another state. The bodies of Bob Sims and of three Savages were taken down Saturday and thrown over the wall into the graveyard.

Sims's family and followers who were lynched that Christmas season were eventually buried in the Sims family cemetery, where their tombstones remain a testimony to the war begun by Bloody Bob Sims.

CHAPTER 2

RUBE BURROW

SON OF A WITCH

R euben Houston Burrow was the son of a witch—or so people said. He was born one of ten children to Allen and Martha "Dame" Terry Burrow near the town of Sulligent in Lamar County, Alabama. Dame Burrow had a reputation for faith healing, and some say she could cure cancer simply by uttering an incantation.

Young Rube, as he was known, was born in 1854 or 1855 and raised on the family farm, along with his siblings, in this atmosphere of superstition where items in the larder might include eye of newt, toe of frog, wool of bat and lizard's leg.

He also witnessed illegal activity and brushes with the law when his father, a Confederate veteran, supplemented his income by becoming a moonshiner. Allen Burrow was indicted in about 1876 for illicit distilling and left the country for two years to avoid arrest. He returned after making a compromise with the federal government and lived a quiet existence in Lamar County.

Portrait of Rube Burrow. *Alabama Department of Archives and History.*

Rube was especially close to his younger brother Jim, born in 1858, and the two were fascinated by tales of Jesse James and his gang of outlaws. One event when Rube was about fifteen foreshadowed his future. The teenager reportedly donned a mask and robbed a neighbor at gunpoint, but his father discovered him and made him return the money. With James as his inspiration, Rube would turn to robbing trains after his attempt to be a farmer and family man failed. He would eventually gain a reputation for violence second only to James himself.

In 1872, when he was about eighteen years old, Rube left the family farm and moved to Stephenville, Texas, to work for his uncle, Joel Burrow, on his cattle ranch. Within three years, Rube married Virginia Alvison, the daughter of prominent rancher H.B. Alvison, and his future as a farmer seemed secure. He and Virginia had two children.

Rube's brother Jim joined him in Texas in 1876, and the two worked as cowboys for a while. In 1880, Rube's young wife died of yellow fever, and unable to care for the children, he took them to Alabama to be raised by his parents. He married Adeline Hoover in 1884 and moved to Alexander, Texas, for a fresh start at farming, but failing crops and a failing marriage led to Rube's change in careers. He and Jim, sometimes called the "Burrow brothers," began careers as criminals.

From 1886 to 1890, the Burrows and their gang robbed express trains in Texas, Alabama, Arkansas, Louisiana and Indian Territory, all the while eluding capture by lawmen and investigators from the Pinkerton National Detective Agency.

By December 1886, Rube and Jim had formed a gang with William L. Brock, Leonard Brock, Henderson Brumley and Nep Thornton with the intention of robbing the Denver & Fort Worth Express when it passed through Bellevue, Texas. However, their inexperience gave passengers time to hide their valuables, and their first haul was only $300. A headline in the December 12, 1886 edition of the *Fort Worth Daily Gazette* said the robbers "fail[ed] to take much of a haul probably through lack of experience in the business."

Just six months later, in June 1887, the gang tried again in Ben Brooks, Texas. This time, the robbers had more success, and Burrow robbed another train at the same spot that September. News accounts estimated the gang got away with as much as $30,000, likely an exaggeration.

Rube was reportedly generous and often sent letters filled with money to his parents.

The robbery that December of the St. Louis, Arkansas & Texas Railroad express train at Genoa, Arkansas, would put Rube Burrow on wanted lists. The train was carrying a Louisiana lottery payoff. After the Arkansas robbery, Pinkerton detectives and lawmen in several states were searching for the Burrow brothers, who, up until then, had no record and were unknown to lawmen.

That would change when a raincoat left behind the day of the robbery was traced to gang member William Brock, who quickly pointed a finger at Burrow, although he said he didn't know Rube's whereabouts. Through a letter Burrow wrote to Brock, detectives learned Rube was in Lamar County, Alabama.

Pinkerton detective John McGinn arrived in Lamar County in January 1888 to arrest Burrow but initially went to the wrong house, giving Jim time to warn Rube. The brothers caught a Louisville & Nashville train near Birmingham, but a conductor recognized them from wanted posters. He sent a wire to the station in Montgomery, and police met the train. A gunfight ensued. Rube shot an officer and escaped; Jim was captured and sent to prison in Little Rock, Arkansas.

Although Jim wrote to his family saying he had a good chance of beating the charges against him, he would not leave jail alive. He died of tuberculosis on October 5, 1888.

Years later, in 1893, the legend of the Burrow brothers would again make news when bodies of convicts buried near the prison were exhumed to be moved to a new cemetery. According to a newspaper account at the time, Jim's coffin was empty when opened. A story in the *Milwaukee Journal* reported, "The discovery of the empty coffin has created a sensation and rumors are in circulation that the bandit may have escaped."

On December 15, 1888, Rube and Leonard Brock, who was using the alias "Joe Jackson," robbed a train in Duck Hill, Mississippi, during which Rube shot and killed a passenger. It was Rube's first murder, and his actions would subsequently grow more reckless.

Burrow and his men returned to Lamar County with the knowledge that Rube's large network of siblings would give them safe haven. Into 1889, they stayed successfully hidden until Rube murdered a well-known and respected local postmaster, Mose Graves. Graves had refused to hand over a package to Rube, thinking it looked suspicious, and Rube shot him. The package contained a wig and false mustache for Rube to change his appearance. By this time, even Lamar County residents were turning against Rube.

Burrow robbed two more trains later in the year and was pursued by Pinkerton detectives who tracked him and Ben Thornton across the Raccoon Mountains in Blount County, Alabama. Newspapers reported that the posse of "forty men" caught up to the outlaws near Brooksville: "The outlaws opened

Left: Illustration of a gun battle with Rube Burrow and Joe Jackson fighting a posse on Sand Mountain in northern Alabama. *From the* New York Sun, *October 12, 1890.*

Below: A historical marker in Flomaton mentions outlaws who came through the area, including Rube Burrow. *Historical Marker Database.*

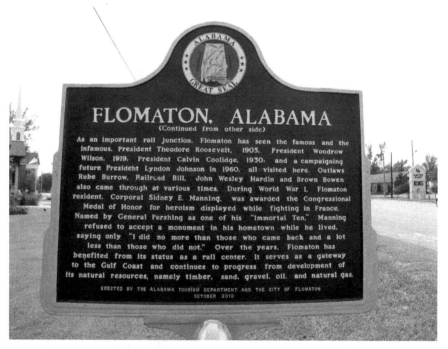

fire, and at the first volley Deputy Sheriffs Henry Anderson and Penwood Ward fell dead, the former shot through the head and the latter through the breast. The officers returned the fire and over 100 shots were exchanged."

Several others in the posse were wounded. The outlaws made their way to a house and eventually escaped, but newspapers carried an account that would add to negative public sentiment against Rube.

Rube Burrow's body was displayed in this coffin following his death. *Public domain.*

The *Bridgeport Morning News* reported on October 28, 1889: "Rube appeared at the door with a woman in front of him, serving as a shield between him and the officers' guns, and replied defiantly that he would die before he would surrender. The officers would not shoot for fear of hitting the woman."

Rube Burrow managed to elude authorities in rural Alabama for another two years. On October 9, 1890, Rube was captured by Jesse Hildreth and Frank Marshall at George Ford's cabin in Marengo County, Alabama.

The outlaw was taken to jail in Linden, Alabama. He soon used his legendary charm to talk his guards into untying his hands and handing him his sack of snacks so he could eat. The sack also contained a pistol, and Rube soon escaped again. But he made a calculated mistake. At the front of the jail, he got in a shootout with local merchant Jefferson Davis Carter. One of Burrow's bullets hit Carter in the stomach, but Carter's shot to Burrow's chest was fatal.

The body of the notorious outlaw was shipped to Lamar County by train. It made several stops along the way to let people view the body. In Birmingham, thousands of people reportedly turned out to view the corpse and snatch souvenirs, such as buttons from his coat, snippets of hair and even his boots.

Rube's father met the train when it arrived in Sulligent. When the coffin was opened to allow him to make positive identification, he reportedly said, "It is Rube."

Rube Burrow was buried in Fellowship Cemetery, where his grave is marked with a simple concrete stone with his name crudely etched on the surface.

CHAPTER 3

RAILROAD BILL

A MAN AND A MYTH

Any outlaw who has caught the public's eye has a legend that surrounds him, but usually those legends do not have the supernatural aspect that one notorious Alabama outlaw's does. History and lore have recorded this outlaw's name as Railroad Bill, and he was active in southern Alabama and northern Florida in the mid-1890s.

Even though Bill was reportedly killed in 1897, Louisville & Nashville Railroad workers to this day report seeing a black man wearing clothes that don't fit our modern times limping along the tracks that run north to south from Alabama into Pensacola, Florida. Many witnesses say the man watches them closely, almost menacingly, but never speaks. If he is watched too long, the mysterious man will walk into a nearby forest and disappear. Railroad employees and locals feel this mysterious spirit is that of Railroad Bill, who, during his time terrorizing the area, never shied away from letting people think that he had supernatural powers. Many mysterious qualities were attributed to Bill in life, including shape-shifting and the ability to disappear and make bloodhounds lose their smell. Others said Bill could only be killed with a silver bullet.

The legend of Railroad Bill began in the winter of 1894, when railroad employees began noticing an African American vagrant illegally riding the trains on the Louisville & Nashville Railroad line in southern Alabama near the Florida line. On March 6, 1895, railroad detectives attempted to restrain the vagrant when they found him sleeping on a water tank along the tracks. During the struggle, the man fired shots at the detectives and hijacked one of the train cars by disconnecting it. As the chase began, the man jumped from the boxcar and disappeared into the surrounding woods.

This incident initiated a manhunt. The railroad detectives gathered a posse and began tracking the man they were now calling Railroad Bill. The posse spent several weeks tracking Bill, and following leads, they finally arrived in Bay Minette, Alabama, on April 6, 1895. Details on what transpired in the town that day are sketchy, but historians report that the posse of about twenty men confronted the man they thought was Railroad Bill and a gunfight broke out. When the gunfight ended, Baldwin County deputy sheriff James Stewart was dead, and Railroad Bill was still on the loose, now wanted for murdering a lawman.

Stewart's killing brought widespread attention to the outlaw, and people began pondering his origins. Railroad Bill was first thought to be a man named Morris Slater, who lived near the town of Teaspoon, Florida (which is now known as Cyprus, Florida), about forty miles north of Pensacola. He worked in a turpentine camp and bragged to co-workers that he had once worked for the railroad and had also worked as a circus performer doing magic tricks under the name Wild Bill McCoy, a name that he still used on occasion.

His time in the turpentine camp was apparently where Slater's life as an outlaw began. Gathering sap to create turpentine was labor intensive and even more so for Slater because he would perform his work with a rifle down his pant leg. This, of course, caught the eye of Escambia County deputy sheriff Allen Brewton, who advised Slater that he had to have a permit to carry the rifle. Slater told him in no uncertain terms that he was not going to get a permit.

A few days after this incident, Deputy Brewton returned to the turpentine camp with three other officers to confront Slater and force him to buy a permit for the gun or to confiscate the weapon. Slater would not cooperate and began to walk away from the officers, so they opened fire on him. Their shots went wide, and Slater returned fire at the officers, shooting off part of the ear of one of the deputies. Slater could not return to his job at the turpentine camp because he was now a wanted man, so he became an outlaw.

In early 1894, Slater began learning his craft by robbing the occasional business establishment, but he discovered that the real loot was found in robbing trains. The loot he took was not always in the form of money; many times he stole goods that could be used by people in the area. Slater would then sell these items to the locals for pennies on the dollar, and in many cases, he would give items to the poor, both black and white. Bill's purported charity made him a popular figure in southern Alabama and northern

Florida. As his fame grew, his identity as Morris Slater began to fade and was replaced by the legend and lore of Railroad Bill.

Railroad Bill was busy robbing as many trains as he could. As the legend of Railroad Bill grew, robberies of every train and business were attributed to him, although he could not possibly have committed them all. The claims only fueled the myth, putting law enforcement officers, railroad security and multiple private detection agencies on his trail.

One tactic used to capture Railroad Bill was to have black detectives go undercover to gain his confidence. One of the most documented investigations of Railroad Bill in late 1894 was carried out by Detective Mark Stinson. Stinson, who was black, was assigned to befriend Bill and gain his confidence. Stinson managed to do so and rode with the outlaw for several months. During this time, he made multiple reports to local officials regarding Bill's actions, but in every report, he noted that Railroad Bill "never let his guard down" so there was no chance for the outlaw to be captured. Eventually, Stinson's reports stopped, and the detective was never heard from again. Authorities believed Railroad Bill had discovered the detective's true purpose, and another murder was attributed to the outlaw.

With his crime spree continuing, Railroad Bill had a price on his head that was steadily growing. Authorities in Mobile posted a $500 reward for information on the capture of Railroad Bill, also known as Morris Slater. Information on Bill began to pour in from locals hoping to collect.

In early July 1895, an informant passed information about Railroad Bill's hideout to Escambia County sheriff E.S. McMillan. The informant advised the sheriff that Bill was holed up outside Bluff Springs and that Bill was heavily armed and always on guard for an attack. Sheriff McMillan raised a posse and, as darkness approached on the night of July 3, 1895, set out to capture or kill the bandit. True to the informant's information, Railroad Bill was ready for the attack, and an immense gun battle ensued between the outlaw and the posse. During the barrage of gunfire, Sheriff McMillan was struck in the chest.

The injury to Sheriff McMillan angered the men in the posse, and they unleashed a torrent of gunfire that they were sure killed the outlaw. They turned their attention to the gravely injured sheriff. Working in the darkness was futile, so the men loaded him on a wagon and took him to a doctor in town, planning to return at first light to collect Railroad Bill's body. They soon learned the sheriff was struck in the heart, and even with medical attention, he soon died, leaving another murdered lawman attributed to Railroad Bill.

When members of the posse returned to the site of the shootout, they were shocked to see there was no body, only a blood trail that trackers eventually lost. The fact that Railroad Bill had survived yet another shootout added to his aura of mystery. Many of the posse members and most civilians began to believe that Railroad Bill could only be killed by a silver bullet.

Even as tales of Railroad Bill's supernatural powers grew, his popularity with residents of the area began to fall dramatically. Sheriff McMillan was a popular lawman, and his death brought about a change in the public opinion of Railroad Bill. People began to see him for what he was—an outlaw. The killing also resulted in a reward of $1,250, a fortune to most people at the time. The promise of the large reward led to the formation of the posse that would finally see the end of Railroad Bill. The posse consisted of local lawmen, bounty hunters from as far away as Texas and Indiana, operatives of the Pinkerton National Detective Agency, L&N detectives and the occasional vigilante. The *Montgomery Daily Advertiser* reported that "those hunting the fugitive had become a small army numbering at least one hundred men loaded for bear."

Several stories surround the death of Railroad Bill, but one detail remains constant. The outlaw was killed on March 7, 1896, on Ashley Street in Atmore, Alabama. The most widespread story of that day says that a posse hunting the outlaw stopped in Atmore to rest the horses at the same time that a black man with a limp entered the Tidmore and Ward store on Ashley Street to purchase cheese and crackers. The shopkeeper recognized the man as Bill McCoy and knew he was wanted, but legends of the outlaw's supernatural abilities kept the businessman from attempting to subdue the man. After paying, Bill exited the store and sat on a barrel outside to eat his cheese and crackers.

J. Leonard McGowan, a member of the posse, also had recognized the outlaw, but remaining members of the group were watering their horses or resting from their travels. McGowan knew he would be unable to win in a gunfight against the killer who had vanquished many a foe, so he entered the store with his rifle and took up a position behind a window with a view of the infamous Railroad Bill.

It was the middle of the afternoon on a clear day in Atmore when Railroad Bill met his demise. McGowan squeezed the trigger of his rifle, firing the round that mortally wounded Bill McCoy, aka Morris Slater, aka Railroad Bill. Less than one second after the outlaw was struck by McGowan's rifle round, his body was struck a second time by buckshot from the shopkeeper's shotgun. The rest of the posse, hearing the gunfire, arrived on the scene and also opened fire on the corpse of Railroad Bill. After years of looting, robbing and murdering along the Alabama-Florida line, the notorious outlaw had finally met his maker at the hands of one of the largest posses ever formed.

His death on the unassuming street in the town of Atmore was not the end of the tale of Railroad Bill. Because the outlaw was so well known and feared, authorities wanted to prove to residents that Railroad Bill had been killed, so his body was put on public display. The body was first displayed in Brewton, Alabama, where hundreds of people came to view it. Curious souvenir hunters even went so far as to pay fifty cents for a photo of McGowan with his rifle standing over Railroad Bill's corpse.

The body remained on display in Brewton for a week before being transported to Montgomery, Alabama, where it attracted thousands of spectators, to be displayed for another week before then being transported to Pensacola, Florida, where even more curious onlookers paid twenty-five cents to view the body. After this stop, Railroad Bill was quietly buried in an unmarked grave outside the city.

The display of Railroad Bill's body around the state was intended to bring an end to his legend, but it did not. After the body had been on display in Brewton, a story took hold in the community that a man who had helped prepare Bill's body for display had been scratched in the process and then died from blood poisoning. At the same time, many residents claimed that the dead man was not Railroad Bill at all. They said that the outlaw continued to live peacefully in the swamps. As late as the Great Depression, people in rural Escambia County would claim Railroad Bill brought them their government assistance food. Other legends say that Bill survived the final gunfight by changing into an animal form and fleeing to the swamps. This form is said to be a fox, an eagle or a hound.

The legacy of Railroad Bill goes beyond tales of the supernatural. History has shown Bill to be a symbol of the social and economic divide in the Deep South after Reconstruction. The years around Bill's crime spree were a time of increasing segregation in Alabama and other southern states. The hunt for Railroad Bill was portrayed by many newspapers as a case of the white establishment determined to capture the black outlaw.

Many innocent African Americans paid the price for the crimes of Railroad Bill. Questionably identified suspects were abducted and brought to town for the captors to claim the reward. Others were arrested and accused without any proof of being accomplices of the outlaw. Many times, those arrested were needlessly beaten, whipped and even killed. The Brewton paper the *Pine Belt News* ran a headline that stated, "The Wrong Man Shot" in relation to a capture of a supposed Railroad Bill. Reports from Florida, Georgia, Mississippi and Texas painted a similarly grim picture of the injustices against those inaccurately targeted as Railroad Bill.

Railroad Bill's effect on the South is evident in popular culture. Blues ballads were recorded about the outlaw in the 1950s and 1960s, many blues musicians took the stage name Railroad Bill and, most famously, the Labor Theater in New York City produced the musical play *Railroad Bill*, written by C.R. Portz.

CHAPTER 4

MOUNTAIN TOM CLARK

DESTINED TO BE WALKED ON

Have you ever heard the phrase "It feels like someone just walked over my grave"? It has a few meanings but is most commonly associated with an unexplained shiver. If anyone knows how this feels, it would be one of north Alabama's most notorious villains. Outlaw Tom Clark is buried under the roadway in the middle of Tennessee Street near the City Cemetery in Florence, Alabama. The people of Florence were so pleased with the idea that they even dedicated a memorial plaque to mark the grave, which reads:

> *The notorious outlaw gang leader who boasted that no one would ever run over Tom Clark lies buried near the center of Tennessee Street where now all who pass by do run over him.*
> *In 1872, Clark, who terrorized helpless citizens during the Civil War, confessed to at least nineteen murders, including a child, and was hanged with two companions. Although graves were already dug in a nearby field, outraged townspeople interred Clark beneath Tennessee Street thus bringing his boast to naught.*

Tom Clark first came to Lauderdale County in either late 1862 or early 1863 and moved into what was known as the Blackburn settlement north of Florence. Locals immediately gave the new man the nickname "Mountain Tom Clark" because there was already a Tom Clark in the area and the stranger had come from a mountainous county. Clark was fleeing to Lauderdale County, on the run from the Confederate conscription law.

"MOUNTAIN" TOM CLARK
HANGED SEPTEMBER 4, 1872
• • •
This notorious outlaw gang leader who boasted that no one would ever run over Tom Clark lies buried near the center of Tennessee Street where now all who pass by do run over him. In 1872 Clark, who terrorized helpless citizens during the Civil War, confessed to at least nineteen murders, including a child, and was hanged with two companions. Although graves were already dug in a nearby field, outraged townspeople interred Clark beneath Tennessee Street thus bringing his boast to nought.

This monument to Mountain Tom Clark was erected near his grave in the middle of Tennessee Street in Florence, Alabama. *Authors' collection.*

Clark was not in Lauderdale County long, though, before the conscription finally caught up with him. It was a cold and disagreeable day. Clark was building a stick chimney for his uncompleted house, in which his wife and child of only a few days of age were ill, when the Confederate authorities took him away from his family and enlisted him in the Confederate army. Many who knew him say this was his breaking point from which the passions of a thousand devils were aroused, and many even go so far as to say the man then became a demon.

Clark saw no need to be in the service of Confederate army and found the Confederate officers to be much too anxious for his services, so at the first opportunity, he fled the camp, making his way north to Clifton, Tennessee, where he then enlisted in the Union army and was assigned to the Second Tennessee Mounted Infantry as a guard. Being a mountain man and good with a rifle, he could have been of great benefit to the army, but his demons had other plans.

When Clark enlisted in the Union army, orders were strict and the discipline rigid. Everything was in confusion, and scouting was the order of the day, as guerrillas and bushwhackers were running amuck. The standing orders at the post were to let all persons enter but let no one under any circumstances pass outside the guard line. A gentleman in the camp spent several days observing Clark and thought him susceptible to being bribed into letting him leave the camp. The man gave Clark a nice pocketwatch to simply turn his back as this gentleman left the camp. Unfortunately, his absence was noticed, and the officers began an investigation. Of course, they would have discovered Clark's complicity in the crime, so he fled the camp, figuring that deserting would be a better outcome than facing a firing squad after a court-martial.

Not long after his departure from the Union army, Clark fell in with what many locals would call one of the worst gangs of cutthroats that ever cursed the face of the earth. People in northwest Alabama called them the Booger Gang. Many of the men were reared in the country and had served in the Confederate army, become deserters and then enlisted in the Federal army only to desert as soon as they could do so with the accoutrements furnished to engage in a series of the most bloody and brutal murders and robberies in American history.

The gang's first true act of violence was in Bainbridge, Tennessee, where Clark went to kill a man by the name of Silas Green. The outlaw had wounded Silas in an earlier fight, but Silas had escaped before Clark could end his life. So the Booger Gang descended on Bainbridge to finish the job. As the armed men were riding up to the cabin where Silas was staying, they came across two Confederate soldiers standing guard by the creek and shot them dead. At the cabin, Clark found another soldier near the door, and even though the soldier was pleading for his life, Clark shot him. After he fell, one of the Booger Gang saw that he was not yet dead and shot him in the chest to finish the job. The men then set fire to Silas's cabin.

While that was the first recorded violent act of the outlaw's reign of terror, it was certainly not the most widely known. In April 1865, Clark and his gang paid a visit to a wealthy old man by the name of John S. Wilson trying to learn where he kept his stash of money. Wilson refused to reveal where the money was hidden, so the gang of men led by Clark cruelly tortured him. They piled books on his chest and burned them, poured burning coals on his feet and, when he again failed to give up the desired information, shot to death the feeble, sick old man.

Matthew Willon Jr., the plantation overseer, happened to come upon the scene of the violence against Mr. Wilson, and he was shot several times and was dead before he hit the ground. The outlaws then looted the plantation, killing a young man by the name of Mr. Twitty in the process. Another young man named Foster was shot but escaped death. Clark later bragged

OUTLAW TOM CLARK.

History of War-Time Terror to North Alabama.

His Final Exploits, Capture and Hanging —A Correct Write-Up of This Fiend.

As a preface to my story, I will say to The Reaper's readers that everything that will not bear the closest investigation has been ignored, because, even of the man who is steeped in crime, the truth is what history de-

the penalty seven years before Clark expiated his crimes.

HIS CROWNING ACTS

were committed in April, 1865, when old man John S. Wilson waa cruelly tortued with fire to make him reveal the hiding place of his money. They piled books on his breast and burned them, poured burning coals on his feet, and failing to procure the desired information, they cruelly shot to death this feeble, sick old man, also Matthew Willon, Jr., the plantation overseer, Mr. Twitty, and wounded a young man named Foster, who saved his life by feigning death. This occurred at the Wilson homestead, where

An article on Tom Clark in the *Times-Daily* newspaper on March 4, 1893. *Public domain.*

that, after these deeds, the gang members danced with glee before they rode roughshod into Florence, where they held high carnival until near the hour when ghosts cease to walk.

Over the next several months in Florence, Clark and his gang tortured several citizens. Among them were Dr. Joseph Milner and John Kackelman; Edmund Poole was also tortured and robbed, and many other outrages were perpetrated against the citizens of Florence.

Eventually, the violence began to catch up to the outlaws, and two of the Booger Gang were caught and shot to death by federal authorities for their many crimes. The two men were ridden out a little way from town on the military road and taken to a little ravine, where a fatal volley was fired. But they had not managed to catch the gang's leader, Tom Clark. That would come seven years later.

Clark had taken refuge for several years in the mountain areas of Jackson County, but in September 1872, he was visiting Waterloo, Alabama, when someone recognized him and reported his whereabouts to Sheriff Ed Blair in Florence. The sheriff gathered a small posse and rode out to Waterloo, where they were able to capture Clark and two other men on Pettypool Hill near Gravelly Springs. The other men happened to be thieves wanted by the State of Indiana. Some legends claim Clark was wearing a woman's dress when he was arrested, but no official accounts confirm the claim.

The trio was taken to the jail on Pine Street in Florence, but as expected, the men did not remain there long. On September 14, 1872, a lynch mob formed, and the outlaws were wrested from the jail and taken a short distance to a lot on the corner of Tombigbee and Pine Streets. There, they were all three hanged from the branches of a large sycamore tree.

After the execution, the ladies of Florence went to the mayor and requested that Clark and the other men not be interred in the consecrated ground of the Florence Cemetery. The mayor agreed, and their bodies were taken to a field across from the cemetery where the two wanted Indiana men were buried. One man in the mob recalled hearing Tom Clark boasting, "No man will ever run over Tom Clark!" So the lynch mob dug up the road and buried his body under Tennessee Street, just outside the gates of the Florence City Cemetery, where his remains still lie.

During his life, Clark was known to have killed sixteen men, but there were probably more unrecorded. Before his death, though, Clark declared that, of all his killings, he only regretted one, and that one murder shows the monster that Tom Clark truly was. The murder victim was a one-year-old boy. The boy had been wearing a medallion Clark wanted, so Clark picked the boy up, impaled him with a knife and took the medallion.

Clark, like all bad men, received credit for crimes he never committed and some that were not committed at all, but those Clark did commit were so fiendish and diabolical that a run-of-the-mill criminal would shudder with horror at the thought of them. And that is why, on that crisp fall evening in 1872, a group of terrorized citizens decided that Tom Clark and the demon inside him should eternally suffer the sensation of someone walking over his grave.

CHAPTER 5

LEWIS POWELL

HISTORY'S MOST HATED WOULD-BE ASSASSIN

In June 1865, the minister's son, barely twenty-one years old, spent his days in a tiny windowless cell with only a mattress and bucket for amenities. But he had no need of a window—his ears and eyes were covered with a padded, canvas hood, leaving only his mouth free to receive enough sustenance to keep him alive until he could be executed.

The stoic Lewis Powell, also known by the alias Lewis Payne or Paine, soon would be free of his earthly prison when he was hanged for his role in one of American history's most hideous and high-profile crimes: the plot to kill President Abraham Lincoln and Secretary of State William H. Seward.

On July 7, 1865, Powell, convicted of repeatedly stabbing Seward in a failed attempt to kill him, was hanged alongside fellow convicted conspirators Mary Surratt, David Herold and George Atzerodt. Powell's story did not end there. It was 127 years later, in 1992, that his skull was discovered amid artifacts at the Smithsonian Museum and buried alongside his parents in Seminole County, Florida.

But how did Powell go from a quiet, unassuming boy to wounded soldier to escaped prisoner of war to assassin?

Lewis Thornton Powell was born in Randolph County, Alabama, on April 22, 1844, to George Cader Powell, a Baptist minister, and Patience Caroline Powell, who were likely second cousins. The youngest of three surviving sons, Lewis was described by some of his eight siblings as shy and well liked. Both George and Patience were educated, which was unusual for a woman of the era. As a girl in Georgia, Patience attended a school for young ladies.

Lewis Powell, who was hanged for taking part in the conspiracy to kill President Lincoln, shown handcuffed aboard the monitor gunboat USS *Saugus*. *Wikimedia Commons.*

While in Alabama, George worked as assistant tax collector and then as tax assessor for Randolph County. While attending services at Liberty Baptist Church in Russell County, George was "called" to the ministry and quit his job in the tax office to preach and work on the farm, operating a small blacksmith business to make additional money.

After George was ordained in 1847, the family moved to Georgia, where he acted as a minister, farmer and local schoolmaster. George Powell educated all his children, and Lewis developed a love of reading and studying. The introverted boy also loved being with the animals on the family farm and became known for his ability to nurse sick animals to health. His family and neighbors began calling him "Doc." On one occasion when Lewis was thirteen, his passion for animals was his undoing. A mule kicked him in the face with enough force to break his jaw. The jaw didn't set correctly, leaving Lewis with a more prominent jut to the left side of his face.

In 1859, when Lewis was fifteen, the family moved again, to Belleville, Florida, as rumblings of the Civil War were beginning to grow louder across the South. Like many young men, including his brothers, Lewis signed up to fight for the Confederacy as soon as possible after the start of hostilities.

John Wilkes Booth.
Wikimedia Commons.

On May 30, 1861, at age seventeen, Lewis enlisted in Company I of the Second Florida Infantry in Jasper, Florida. It was the last time the Reverend George Powell saw his son alive. Lewis would fight with honor in numerous battles, including those at Fredericksburg, Chancellorville, Second Manassas and Antietam. During this time, he grew into a man, reaching six feet, one inch in height. Despite his slightly crooked jawline, Lewis was a handsome man with blue eyes and dark hair.

Lewis was at the Battle of Gettysburg when, on the second day of fighting, he was shot in the wrist, shattering bone. He was taken as a prisoner of war at the hospital at Pennsylvania College on July 2, 1863, and was later transferred to a Baltimore, Maryland hospital, where he befriended a volunteer nurse named Maggie Branson, who was thirty-one years old. Lewis escaped the hospital, probably with Maggie's help, and fled to Alexandria,

David Herold. *Wikimedia Commons.*

Virginia, where he joined Colonel John Singleton Mosby's cavalry in the fall of 1863. Sometime in 1864, Lewis joined the Confederate Secret Service.

He returned to Baltimore on January 13, 1865, to visit Maggie Branson's boardinghouse. At this time, he also met a fellow Secret Service operative, John Surratt, who would later be involved in the conspiracy to assassinate Lincoln. Surratt, in turn, introduced Powell to John Wilkes Booth.

An illustration of Lewis Powell fighting Frederick Seward. *Wikimedia Commons.*

After crossing Union lines to return to Baltimore, Lewis told Union troops he had deserted his regiment and agreed to sign an oath of allegiance. He signed as "Lewis Paine," later written "Payne" in court and media accounts.

After weeks of discussing a possible kidnapping, the final details of the assassination plot were hashed out in Lewis's room at the Kirkwood Hotel in Baltimore, where Booth assigned roles to Powell, George Atzerodt and David Herold the night of April 13.

Powell was assigned to take Herold and kill Seward at his Washington, D.C. home. Atzerodt was assigned to assassinate Vice President Andrew Johnson, and Booth was to assassinate President Lincoln.

Powell's assignment was made easier by the fact that Seward had been badly injured on April 5 in a carriage accident and was suffering a concussion, broken jaw and broken arm. He was convalescing at his home when, on the night of April 14, Powell knocked on the door of the Seward home, saying he was delivering medication from Dr. Tullio Suzarro Verdi.

Lewis encountered Seward's son Frederick on the stairs and pistol-whipped him with his 1858 Whitney revolver before stepping into the room where Seward was bedridden and stabbing the secretary of state several times with a silver-mounted Bowie knife in his neck and face. One wound went through Seward's cheek, but a splint on his broken jaw helped save his life by protecting his jugular vein.

Accounts vary on others in the home who were attacked, but the injured likely included Seward's sons Augustus and Frederick; his military nurse, Sergeant George F. Robinson; and a messenger, Emerick Hansell, who arrived at the home just as Powell was running into the night, certain he had mortally wounded his target. He would learn following his arrest the next day that Seward had survived.

Lewis discarded the knife and made it back to his getaway horse, which had been bought by Booth the previous December. At some point, he either abandoned the horse or was thrown, because it was found wandering near the Lincoln Branch Barracks near the Capitol.

Lewis hid in a tree for three days before making his way back to Mary Surratt's boardinghouse. When he arrived, he saw Mrs. Surratt being arrested on a charge of conspiracy to assassinate Lincoln. Lewis, too, was arrested. By this time, Lewis knew his attempt to kill Seward had failed, Booth's attempt to kill Lincoln had succeeded and George Atzerodt had gotten drunk, lost his nerve and never tried to kill Johnson.

The conspirators would also learn that, rather than being hailed as heroes of the Southern cause, as Booth had hoped, they were vilified. Booth was shot to death by soldiers twelve days after assassinating Lincoln, while the others faced trial.

Seward family servant William Bell picked Lewis from a police lineup as the man who carried out Seward's attack. Lewis was confined aboard the monitor gunboat USS *Saugus* and later transferred with surviving conspirators to the Old Arsenal Penitentiary.

Lewis, who was held in a cell seven and a half feet long by four feet wide, was said to be stoic during his incarceration. He was tried under the name "Payne" by a military tribunal and was represented by William E. Doster, who was a Yale and Harvard graduate and former District of Columbia provost marshal. But Doster was fighting an uphill battle. Evidence against Lewis was overwhelming, including proof of his association with Booth and his identification by Bell. Thirty-two witnesses were called to testify against him during the trial.

Doster tried various arguments, first claiming Lewis was insane at the time of the assassination attempt and later that Lewis was acting as a soldier and following orders. During the trial, Lewis's demeanor was described as calm and "like a statue."

In the end, Lewis was found guilty of conspiracy to commit murder and treason and sentenced to death by hanging, as were Atzerodt, Herold and Mary Surratt.

Mary's son, John Surratt, would be tried later in civilian court because of new laws. He was released from prison after a mistrial. He would marry, have seven children and live to be seventy-two years old, dying in 1916.

Lewis gave no excuses for his actions, saying only, "I believed it was my duty."

According to some sources, Lewis's stoic and unapologetic nature led to his further punishment. While other prisoners had the hoods over their heads removed after several days, Lewis's was left in place because guards believed it did not bother him.

However, as the trial neared its end, Lewis was allowed to walk about the prison grounds for an hour each day for exercise. It was on these walks

Execution of the Lincoln conspirators. *LewisPowell.com.*

that Lewis is believed to have gathered the morning glory and larkspur he pressed between the pages of his Bible.

Lewis's early biblical teachings seemed to stay with him until the end. On July 7, 1865, the day of his execution, Lewis spent time in prayer with the Reverend Dr. Abram D. Gillette of First Baptist Church in Washington. He also said he wanted to hear the hymn "The Convert's Farewell." The lyrics are:

> *Farewell, farewell to all below,*
> *The Savior calls and I must go;*
> *I launch my boat upon the sea,*
> *This land is not the land for me,*
>
> *Chorus:*
> *This world is not my home*
> *This world is not my home*
> *This world is all wilderness*
> *This world is not my home*

I've found the winding paths of sin,
A rugged road to travel in;
Beyond the swelling waves I see,
The land my Savior bought for me
(Chorus)

O, sinner, why will you not go?
There's room enough for you I know;
Our boat is sound, the passage free,
And there's a better land for thee
(Chorus)

Farewell, dear friends, I may not stay,
The home I seek is far away;
Where Christ is not, I can not be,
This land is not the land for me.
(Chorus)

Gillette later reported that Lewis sent word to his family through his attorney that he had made peace with God. Gillette wrote that Lewis broke down and cried for the first time since he was sentenced to die because he was overwhelmed by the grief he had caused his mother and father.

"My course is run," Lewis told Gillette. "I know now how foolish, vain and wholly useless it is and must have been, and were I set at liberty this morning, I should hope to be dead by sunset, as all men must hereafter point at me as a murderer."

On execution day, Lewis calmly went to the gallows. Although guards said Lewis never begged for his own life, they claimed he did assert that Mary Surratt was innocent and should not be hanged.

Reverend Gillette thanked the guards for their good treatment of Lewis.

Hangman Christian Rath reportedly remarked, "I hope you die quick" as he placed the noose on Lewis's neck because he was impressed by the young man's courage. But it was not to be.

When the floor dropped from beneath the four conspirators, Lewis's body swung wildly. Mary Surratt died instantly, and Herold died after a brief shudder. Neither Atzerodt's nor Lewis's necks broke on impact, and they hung for several minutes before dying, with Lewis drawing the last breath.

Execution of the Lincoln conspirators. *LewisPowell.com.*

ON A CRISP, sunny November afternoon in 1994, the earthly remains of Lewis Thornton Powell were finally laid to rest. After his skull was discovered in 1992 amid artifacts at the Smithsonian Institute, scientists researched claims by his nearest kin, Helen Alderman, and eventually released the skull to her for burial.

Alderman wanted to bury Lewis's skull next to his parents' graves in Geneva Cemetery in Seminole County, Florida. Powell's casket, first buried near the gallows at a Washington arsenal but later moved to a cemetery in the capital, was removed in the early 1880s when the cemetery land was sold. Researchers believe a funeral home director kept the skull as a souvenir, later giving it to the army's medical museum. The army museum transferred the skull to the Smithsonian on May 7, 1898, where it was stored for nearly one hundred years.

CHAPTER 6

THE NOTORIOUS BART THRASHER

On the night of September 15, 1896, citizens of Alabama breathed a collective sigh of relief as word circulated that one of the most heinous outlaws in the state's short history had been killed the previous night, ending a streak of vengeance murders that shocked the state. That outlaw's name was Bart Thrasher, and word of his death was national news, reaching newspapers as far away as Utica, New York.

Little is known about the early life of the man who would become the notorious Bart Thrasher. His death certificate indicates that he was born in 1869 but does not list a specific date. Records show that he was the eldest of six children born to John Emerson Thrasher and Ruth Jane Vining Thrasher.

History indicates that Bart Thrasher was a typical child growing up in the postwar Reconstruction South, a time when the abject poverty of citizens led more than one young man to turn to the gun to make a living. Thrasher's name was associated with some of the most notable outlaws in the state of Alabama: Doc Panther and brothers Jim and Jack Morrison, to name just a few.

After the so-called King of the Outlaws Rube Burrow was killed in 1890, Alabamians declared that Bart Thrasher had taken Rube's place as the most vicious and wanted outlaw alive. Over the next six years, this sentiment proved to be true.

Thrasher and various gang members became the most feared men in Bibb County, Alabama, which was given the moniker "Bloody Bibb" because it felt to many like the Wild West. Gangs of outlaws and bandits roamed freely, stealing cattle, cotton and valuables and killing anyone who got in their way. At the same time, the county was growing, particularly West Blocton, thanks to the Blocton Mines controlled by the Tennessee Coal, Iron and Railroad Company. At its peak, the town of West Blocton boasted a population of twelve thousand people.

Thrasher had been arrested multiple times in the early 1890s and had twice escaped from penitentiaries. One of the escapes was made with friend Jim Morrison, another famous outlaw. Not long after, in 1895, Morrison was ambushed and killed by Jefferson County deputy sheriff Henry Cole. News of Morrison's death upset Thrasher, who swore vengeance on the deputies who killed his friend.

In 1895, Thrasher was recaptured near Horse Creek, Alabama, and was sentenced to do hard time in the Pratt Mines, a common labor-intensive punishment of the day. Together with nine other men, Thrasher used dynamite to blast a hole in a mine wall to escape through an adjacent mine. Six of the men were soon rounded up by a sheriff's posse, but four of the men, including Thrasher, remained at large.

It did not take long for Thrasher to return to his illegal exploits, as reported by the *Marietta Daily Leader* on January 2, 1896:

> *Bart Thrasher, the notorious Bibb county outlaw, who, with six other convicts, recently broke out of the Pratt mine's penitentiary and, overpowering the guards, escaped, turned up at Horse Creek with an unknown pal, and had a night of robbing and murdering.*
>
> *Ben Adair and a farmer named Jones, while returning home, were held up by Thrasher and his pal, who wore masks and carried pistols, Jones threw up his hands when commanded to do [so], but Adair resisted, when Thrasher shot him dead. The living and dead were then robbed. An hour later the outlaws held up Watchman Davis at Ivy mines and secured his cash and watch. Later on they robbed two miners near Victor mines and concluded by robbing two others at May Ellen mines. The watchman saw Thrasher remove the mask from his face and recognized him. The people around Horse Creek are greatly excited over the night's events, and a strong posse, heavily armed, are searching for the desperadoes, who are in hiding in the mountains and swear they will not be taken alive.*

Adair is the third man Thrasher has killed. For the murder of a Bibb county farmer seven years ago he served a term in prison. Last spring he killed a Negro at Horse creek, for which murder he was serving a ten years' sentence when he escaped. Thrasher is a pal of the late Jim Morrison, the Bibb county outlaw, who was killed last summer by Deputy Sheriff Cole, after having escaped from the penitentiary, and is the most desperate criminal in Alabama. He has escaped from prison three times and twice when recaptured had been shot before he could be secured.

Not long after these escapades, on January 21, 1896, Bibb County sheriff M.J. Latham and Deputy Cole formed a posse after receiving information about Thrasher's travels. The posse hid in the bushes along the road where Thrasher was supposed to pass and waited for the outlaw. It was not long before a man on horseback with a Winchester rifle slung over his back appeared on the road. As he passed the hidden men, the posse emerged from the bushes, and Latham and Cole ordered the man to throw up his hands. The man reached for his gun, and members of the posse fired several shots, killing the man thought to be Bart Thrasher.

Once the dust cleared and the lawmen were able to look at the body, they discovered that it was not Bart Thrasher. The dead man was Bart's brother Elisha Emerson Thrasher, known as Lish Thrasher, who was also a wanted outlaw. The news of his brother's death devastated an already unstable Thrasher, and once again, he swore vengeance on the lawmen responsible.

In late August 1896, Thrasher began carrying out his threats of vengeance. He and another man rode into the town of West Blocton, found Griffin Bass and shot him dead in the street in front of Harvey's Drug Store. Bass was the town's first police officer and had been a part of the posse that killed Lish Thrasher. After gunning down Bass, Thrasher and his partner went to the homes of various lawmen in the posse and pinned notes to their pillows telling each that they were next.

Thrasher's threats frightened the citizens of Bibb County and the lawmen who were called upon to protect them. Thrasher had already killed more than a dozen men, and now he was threatening law officers in their homes. He needed to be stopped. Several posses were formed, but Thrasher seemed to stay one step ahead of them and recruited more men to ride with him.

Cole, who many called the bravest law officer in Alabama, again came to help after Thrasher was spotted near Calera, where he brashly told people to report his whereabouts to the lawmen. Cole obtained information on Thrasher's possible route of travel and, along with another deputy, waited under a bridge for the outlaw to pass. Once Thrasher and his partner were on the bridge, Cole stepped out and ordered the men to throw up their hands. When they did not, the two deputies opened fire on the criminals, killing them.

This time, one of the dead men was indeed identified as the notorious Bart Thrasher. The man riding with him was identified as Doc Panther, another wanted Bibb County outlaw. The man referred to in some newspaper accounts as "the most desperate outlaw in the state" would commit no more crimes. The deaths of Thrasher and Panther marked the seventeenth and eighteenth kills for Cole during his law enforcement career, which gave residents some hope that peace had finally come to Bloody Bibb County.

By the time of his death, Bart Thrasher was a household name in Alabama after he and his gang of outlaws had spent fifteen years cutting a path of thievery, destruction, robbery and death through the area. The span marked more than half of the young outlaw's life.

CHAPTER 7

THE MORRISON BOYS AND JESSE MILLER OF BIBB COUNTY

THE MORRISONS

Jim Morrison and his brothers helped fuel the county's reputation as "Bloody Bibb." Jim and siblings Jack, Sam and Will were part of a gang known as the Morrison Boys who terrorized the county in the 1880s and '90s. At least one newspaper article referred to Jim as Bart Thrasher's partner, but most historians believe the Morrison brothers were a gang unto their own.

They were born to William Morrison, a farmer in the Bibb County community known as Kingdom Beat because its residents supposedly lived like kings. Of a reported eight brothers, at least four became outlaws, with Jim as their leader, despite the fact that he was the middle brother.

The brothers were accused of committing crimes ranging from stealing horses to robbing carriages to murder. By 1891, when Jim would have been about thirty years old, he, Sam, Will and Jack were all fugitives from the law. That December, according to some accounts, Will Morrison was killed by members of another Bibb County gang, this one led by Jesse Miller.

Jim and some of his brothers were captured more than once between 1891 and January 1894, when newspaper accounts report Jim and five other prisoners, likely including some of Morrison's brothers, escaped from the Pratt Mines in Birmingham, where they were forced to work during their prison sentences.

The *Hamilton Free Press* in Marion County reported on January 25, 1894:

Jim Morrison, a notorious desperado from Bibb County, and five other prisoners escaped from Pratt Mines one day last week by cutting their way from one mine to another. Dynamite was used to blow down gates in the mines. Morrison and another prisoner were overtaken by Deputy Sheriff Dexter, of Bibb County, when a fight ensued. Dexter was killed. This is the third time Morrison has escaped from the mines.

An account of the same incident in the *Tennessee Republican* reported a guard named John Patton was "blown up and seriously hurt" in the explosion and that one of the convicts was killed along with Dexter, adding that "the others escaped but officers with dogs are in pursuit." The newspaper also reported that a stash of guns someone left for the convicts allowed them to kill Dexter and escape.

Dexter's death and Jim's frequent escapes made him a much-wanted man.

It took more than a year for lawmen to run Jim Morrison to ground, finally cornering him in Jefferson County in March 1895. Deputy Sheriff Henry Cole had learned Morrison was using the name Johnson and staying at the home of someone named Vines at the fork of the Warrior and Little Warrior Rivers. Cole planned an ambush for the desperado.

The *Hamilton News Press* reported:

Deputy Cole, in company with John Hubbard, lay on the road until Morrison was seen approaching. Hubbard then withdrew into the woods. When Morrison was within about thirty yards Deputy Cole ordered him to throw up his hands. Instead of doing so he began to bring his gun from "right shoulder" to "ready." The officer fired and Morrison fell, pierced by five large buckshot. He lingered about five hours after being shot. The body was carried to Birmingham, where it was seen by two of his brothers and fully identified.

In August 1896, the *Times-Daily* in Florence reported Bart Thrasher was on the lam and "was hounded on all sides by men anxious to make a reward off him and he became desperate and only looks to the future to avenge the death of his father and brother." The article also reports Thrasher's reaction to news of Morrison's death:

A few years ago Thrasher had as his partner another desperado by the name of Jim Morrison. Morrison was a tough man and escaped several times also from the penitentiary. A large reward was offered for his arrest or for his dead body.

Deputy Sheriff Henry Cole of Birmingham, one of the bravest officers in the state, went after the desperado by himself. The latter got information that Morrison was to pass a certain road at a certain time and so laid [sic] for him. Sure enough Morrison was seen to come along the road near where Cole stood behind some bushes.

When [Morrison was] almost on him, Cole ordered the desperado to throw up his hand. Morrison attempted to use his gun and Cole filled him full of lead. Morrison lived a few hours. Thrasher made a threat then that he would avenge the death of his partner.

On September 14, 1896, Thrasher would also be killed.

The deaths of two of Bloody Bibb's most violent outlaws could not bring a close to the era of terror. Jim's surviving brothers continued their criminal ways, running stolen horses through Perry and Hale Counties.

JESSE MILLER

Jesse Miller, born in 1848 as one of seven children to Jesse and Edith Kornegay Miller, was another outlaw who contributed to the nickname "Bloody Bibb." Miller likely crossed paths with Bart Thrasher and Jim Morrison and was known to have made Will Morrison an unwitting accomplice to murder. In March 1891, Jesse asked Will to bring Edmond Parker, a black man, to Schultz Creek Bridge. Will was unaware the men planned to savagely murder Parker.

That August, Miller and gang members Charles Cook and Ike Miller were accused in the vicious murder of well-known Bibb County farmer Henry Smith.

Lawmen would make headway in regaining control of the county in the first week of August when they captured not only Miller but also Jim Morrison.

An August 9, 1891 article in the *Times-Picayune* described the incident:

The excitement in Bibb county over the recent murders, principally that of Henry Smith, a prominent farmer who was tied to a tree and shot to death two weeks ago, continues unabated. To-day Ike Miller, colored, was arrested at Blocton and is in jail for alleged complicity in the murder. On

Monday Jesse Miller and Charles Cook, alleged principals in the murder, will have a preliminary hearing at Centreville before the justice of the peace. Lawlessness has reigned supreme in Bibb for many weeks, and it is expected an effort will be made Monday to rescue Miller and Cook. To thwart this the law and order league sent a committee here to-day to purchase rides and ammunition. It is reported that Jim Morrison, a notorious escaped convict and triple murderer at large in Bibb, was caught by a posse of citizens near Blocton to-day.

In December 1891, either while Miller was in jail or in hiding, four members of his gang lured Will Morrison, a witness to Parker's murder, with a promise of $200 in hush money and murdered him, as well.

A third Morrison brother, Sam, was with Will the night of the shooting but got away. He would avenge his brother's death but not by violent means. Sam testified against Miller in court, resulting in a murder indictment.

It is unclear how Miller was freed from jail, but he became a fugitive and transferred his Scottsville farm to his wife, Amanda Dover—whose brother Pete Dover was Miller's partner in crime—and their daughter, Grace. Jesse and Amanda also had two sons, Brooks and Sterling.

By 1900, Jesse Miller had disappeared, never to be seen again. His date and place of death are unknown.

CHAPTER 8

JOSEPH SANDERS

THE TURNCOAT OF DALE COUNTY

In the town of Newton in Dale County in the southern reaches of the state is a small memorial commemorating what, at the time, was only a minor skirmish in the latter days of the Civil War. The memorial is dedicated to members of the home guard who defended the town against Confederate officer turned Union officer turned bushwhacker Colonel Joseph Sanders.

Joseph Ganes Sanders was reportedly born on December 15, 1827, in South Carolina but moved to Dale County, Alabama, during his childhood. Prior to the outbreak of the Civil War, Sanders was a farmer and millwright in the rural county near the town of Newton. Sanders was known to be a hard worker and was trusted and liked by his neighbors.

With the outbreak of the Civil War, Sanders joined the Confederate army to fight for its cause. Sanders's twelve-month enlistment was confirmed on October 5, 1861, for which he was assigned to the Thirty-first Georgia Infantry. In his time in the unit, Sanders was known to be well liked and earned several promotions before his reenlistment in April 1862 with the rank of sergeant, a rank that guaranteed him a cash signing bonus. Along with the bonus came a thirty-day furlough, during which Sanders returned to his home in Dale County.

When he returned to the unit in May 1862, Sanders was elected to be the captain of his company. Over the next seven months, Sanders led his men in numerous excursions, including the Seven Days' Battles, the Second Battle of Bull Run and the Battle of Antietam, in which he was injured. His injuries kept him sidelined from the war for about a month in December 1862. In

The Civil War memorial in Newton, Alabama. *Wikimedia Commons.*

January 1863, Sanders returned to his command and accompanied the army to Port Royal, Virginia, where his service continued until July after fighting in the Battle of Gettysburg. During this deployment, Sanders's health had begun to decline, and he was unable to serve with his unit. He took a furlough from the army beginning October 9, 1863, and returned home.

There, he began construction of a gristmill, which was much needed because the area was described by one neighbor as being "quite destitute of mills." Sanders once again established himself as a hard worker, and his mill was welcomed by the community. His neighbors valued Sanders's contributions to the community, so they gathered together and drafted a petition to Confederate president Jefferson Davis asking for Sanders to be allowed to resign his military commission and remain at home.

Thirty-two residents signed the petition, saying that Sanders was "patriotic and loyal, and it was his ill health and shattered constitution that kept him away from his command." One of the signers of the petition was Dale County probate judge Daniel Carmichael, whose own son was a Confederate veteran who had also served in the Battle of Antietam, at which Sanders had originally been injured.

President Davis sent the request on to his military commanders to handle. Sanders's regimental commander, Colonel Clement A. Evans, recommended approval of the petition, writing:

Knowing Captain Sanders thoroughly, I can safely assert that the service will be greatly benefitted by his being removed from his present position. The First Lieutenant of the Company is a good officer, in every way competent to hold the Captaincy. It is thought that, perhaps, Captain Sanders may render more material service to the Confederate States, by resuming his former occupation. It is therefore hoped that he will be permitted to return to his home.

Sanders's petition continued up the command ladder, and his resignation was completed on January 29, 1864. It seemed a fitting end to a respectable military career. What would happen only a few months later would shock the small community and leave friends and neighbors wondering what could make Joseph Sanders do the unthinkable: join the Federal army.

The U.S. Army mustered the First Florida Cavalry in August 1864, and among the soldiers assigned to the regiment was Second Lieutenant Joseph Sanders, who had enlisted at Barrancas, Florida, for a three-year term of service.

It was not common for soldiers to switch sides during the war, but it did happen. However, it was very rare for a soldier to receive an officer's commission in both armies. On an interesting note, Sanders's Federal military papers say that he was commissioned from "civil life" and did not make a mention of his time as an officer for the Confederate States.

Dale County locals were trying to figure out what would make Sanders switch sides, and many seemed to think that he was facing conscription back into the Southern army. Others were surprised that Sanders had entered the service because he had supposedly fallen in with a gang of Southern deserters and Unionists who were quietly terrorizing communities throughout lower Alabama.

Sanders's unlawful raiding soon would become evident in his actions as a member of the Union cavalry. While he performed his duties well when he initially joined the service, he veered into the realm of outlaw starting in February 1865. He had been ordered to take twenty men and proceed past Santa Rosa Island in Florida, where he should recruit new soldiers for his regiment and confiscate livestock belonging to "rebel civilians" living in Walton and Holmes Counties in northern Florida. Sanders was given two weeks to accomplish this mission, but he would not return to his commanders in Pensacola for four months.

Instead of following orders, Sanders took his men into the Forks of the Creek Swamp near the community of Campbellton, Florida, where the soldiers hid and planned a raid on the town of Newton, which was the seat of Dale County.

Late in the Civil War, outlaw bands, typically known as "bushwhackers," began attacking, looting and burning county courthouses throughout the South. The Coffee County Courthouse in nearby Elba had recently been attacked and burned by a bushwhacker unit under the command of John Ward, and Sanders had hoped to use the same tactic in Newton. Sanders apparently wanted to burn the courthouse because it contained the war records of Sanders and those of his men, stating that they had served in the Confederate army.

With his plan formed, Sanders and his men left the swamp, setting out for Newton on the night of March 14, 1865. Little did he know that the unit's movement had been detected and word sent ahead to the town warning that an attack was imminent.

Knowledge of the approaching soldiers reached a local Confederate veteran, and he proceeded to the town and gathered the men known as the "home guard," a small cavalry contingent, to stop the intruders. In a small twist of fate, this man was Jesse Carmichael, who had lost his hand fighting at the Battle of Sharpsburg and whose father was Probate Judge Daniel Carmichael, who had signed the petition to have Sanders released from Confederate service.

The home guard commander, Captain Joseph Breare, insisted on taking charge of the town's defense. He commanded his forces along with Carmichael to gather on the courthouse square to repel the raiders when they reached that point. Carmichael knew this was not a good strategy and set out with some of his friends, determined to meet the soldiers on the outskirts of town, giving the home guard time to muster a better defense or for the townspeople to flee the incoming invasion. Carmichael's group met another small group of men with the same idea; together they consisted of ten men.

The men set up picket defenses on the east side of the town and waited for the raiders to arrive. Sanders's regiment included forty-four heavily armed soldiers. Knowing they were outnumbered, Carmichael set up an ambush for the attacking force.

As the mounted men rode into town, one contingent of Carmichael's men let the soldiers pass in the darkness, heading straight for the other contingent. Once Sanders's soldiers passed, Carmichael and the first group of men opened fire on the rear of Sanders's forces. Simultaneously, the second group of men opened fire on the front of the attacking forces, catching them in crossfire.

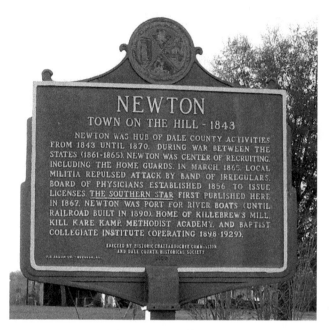

NEWTON
TOWN ON THE HILL - 1843

NEWTON WAS HUB OF DALE COUNTY ACTIVITIES
FROM 1843 UNTIL 1870. DURING WAR BETWEEN THE
STATES (1861-1865), NEWTON WAS CENTER OF RECRUITING,
INCLUDING THE HOME GUARDS. IN MARCH, 1865, LOCAL
MILITIA REPULSED ATTACK BY BAND OF IRREGULARS.
BOARD OF PHYSICIANS ESTABLISHED 1856 TO ISSUE
LICENSES. THE SOUTHERN STAR FIRST PUBLISHED HERE
IN 1867. NEWTON WAS PORT FOR RIVER BOATS (UNTIL
RAILROAD BUILT IN 1890). HOME OF KILLEBREW'S MILL,
KILL KARE KAMP, METHODIST ACADEMY, AND BAPTIST
COLLEGIATE INSTITUTE (OPERATING 1898-1929).

ERECTED BY HISTORIC CHATTAHOOCHEE COMMISSION
AND DALE COUNTY HISTORICAL SOCIETY

This historical marker
in Newton mentions
the raid by Colonel
Joseph Sanders.
Authors' collection.

The attack was devastating to the Union soldiers, and to make matters worse for them, when they attempted to return fire, their guns often misfired. They were surprised, confused and afraid, causing them to break their formation and scatter into the nearby forests. Sanders attempted to rally his men, but with the confusion of the very short battle, it was a near impossible task.

At the end of the battle, the courthouse had been saved, and the much superior Union force under the command of Sanders had been defeated by a group of civilians outnumbered four-to-one, fighting on foot and in the dark. Carmichael's force of ten suffered no casualties or injuries, while Sanders's losses were recorded as three dead and five wounded. The home guard forces under the command of Captain Breare did not fire a shot during the skirmish.

With the defeat at Newton, Sanders did not make another attempt to take the town. His band of bushwhackers spent the next couple of months making small raids into isolated communities and farms in the areas of southern Alabama and northwestern Florida. In June 1865, he finally returned to his headquarters in Pensacola with only eight of his original twenty men.

On his return, Sanders was accused of desertion, considered a capital offense by the U.S. Army and punishable by death. He was also accused of having "become a terror to the people of West Florida" with his "armed gang of deserters." When confronted with these charges, Sanders asserted that an enemy force of seven hundred, sickness among his troops, sore feet, lack of provisions and rising floodwaters all conspired to delay his return to headquarters in the commanded time.

Military leaders did not believe these stories, having heard conflicting stories from area civilians, but they were unable to disprove Sanders's explanation. With great reluctance, officials eventually exonerated Sanders of the charges. On July 20, 1865, Sanders resigned his commission in the U.S. Army, citing concerns for his family's safety and welfare because they were still living in Dale County.

The accusations against Sanders helped his superiors easily make the decision to accept his resignation for the "good of the service."

In making his recommendation for the resignation's approval, Brigadier General Asboth added this statement: "In consideration of the mitigating circumstances and the fact that several other statements given by citizen and soldiers relative to Lieutenant Sanders' prolonged absence involve no criminality, but show gross neglect and incompetency to fill a position of a commissioned officer, I thought it best to recommend the acceptance of his resignation for the good of the service."

Sanders's resignation from the United States Army was effective on September 13, 1865, and he returned home to Dale County, where he planned to resume his gristmill work. However, his actions against the city, county and citizens were not forgotten. Immediately after his return, a posse of locals under the leadership of George Echol went to Sanders's house to arrest the outlaw. Sanders told the men that he would kill anyone who approached his house. Echol underestimated Sanders's resolve and was shot dead upon approaching the house. This broke the spirit of the posse, whose members opted not to challenge Sanders any further.

Knowing that he was no longer welcome in Dale County, Sanders left his family and fled the state of Alabama. He took up residence in a rural part of Dekalb County, Georgia. He again built a small gristmill and seemed to have escaped his past and his Dale County enemies. He lived and worked in the rural area for about a year and a half until he was killed on February 19, 1867, outside the city of Decatur, Georgia.

It has never been confirmed, but rumors abound that the murder of the turncoat Joseph Sanders was committed by Dale County probate judge Abel Echol, the father of George Echol, who had spent more than a year tracking the outlaw. No charges were ever brought against the judge for the outlaw's death.

CHAPTER 9

GALE H. WAGES AND THE LEGEND OF BURIED GOLD

By 1837, people in southern parts of Alabama and Mississippi knew the name Gale Wages. Wages and his cohort, Charles "Preacher" McGrath, traveled the South, posing as preachers before stealing, burning and killing their way into several sacks of gold.

But some might say 1837 was the year Gale Wages went from well-known outlaw to the stuff of legend with one act: burning the courthouse in Americus, Mississippi. The twenty-three-year-old Wages was contacted by Rebecca Wells Copeland of Jackson, Mississippi, who asked for his help. Her fourteen-year-old son, Jim, was facing incarceration on a larceny charge, accused of making repeated trips across the state line to Mobile, Alabama, where he would steal hogs and sell them. Mrs. Copeland, who knew of Wages's reputation through her husband, Isham, was hoping the outlaw could keep Jim out of jail.

Wages formed a plan. He would waylay and kill the hog farmer to prevent him from testifying. He quickly discarded that notion for a better idea.

One evening after dark, Wages rode into the sleepy, sparsely populated farming village of Americus, the Jackson County seat. The unpretentious people of Americus spent their leisure time watching the town's team play baseball, seeing who could climb a greased pole fastest and holding picnics each summer.

They had no way of knowing that, after Gale Wages and his new friend Jim rode into town, the fate of Americus would be sealed.

With Jim's help, Wages burned the county courthouse, destroying any evidence against young Jim, along with most every other record of the county's history. Within a couple of decades, the town's population dwindled and the county seat moved to Pascagoula. Americus was no more.

That was none of Gale Wages's concern. He'd guaranteed the freedom of the young scoundrel and accepted him into his gang. Together, along with Preacher McGrath, they would form one of the most notorious outlaw gangs in the South, and it soon would take the name of the teen outlaw: the James Copeland Gang.

Argelius "Gale" Wages was born in about 1814 to Jacob and Susannah Wages, who came from South Carolina to settle in Washington County, then part of the Mississippi Territory. Jacob and Susannah started a farm on Big Creek Swamp, about twenty-five miles outside the port city of Mobile. They brought with them four children: Elizabeth "Betsy" Wages, Jacob, Rebecca Racy and Gale, the youngest. Their new home, known as Big Creek Place, was a large farm, and at one point, Jacob had as many as thirteen slaves.

By the time he was in his teens, Gale was getting into trouble. He was known to steal mules and horses, but when he teamed with Preacher McGrath, the two young men developed a scam.

They would visit a small town and either Gale or McGrath would pose as an evangelical preacher and advertise a revival. Most small-town residents in the untamed territory would attend church any time someone pulled out a Bible, and while the townspeople were singing hymns, the second man would loot as many homes and businesses as possible.

After Wages and McGrath accepted young James Copeland into the gang in 1837, it became known as the Wages-Copeland Gang and eventually the James Copeland Gang, which, at its height, boasted sixty members. If the law got on their trail, members would appear at Big Creek Place, and Old Man Wages, as Jacob Wages was known, would let them hide out on the farm.

Not all of the Wages children turned to crime. Gale's elder sister Betsy married Lloyd Butler and became a well-respected midwife and founding member of Union Primitive Baptist Church. She and her husband moved to Covington County and raised seventeen children.

In 1845, the thirty-one-year-old Wages took time from his thieving to marry the daughter of gang member Allen Brown, Nancy Elizabeth Brown, who was about fifteen years his junior.

Gale didn't honeymoon for long. The gang was soon back to its usual crime spree, reportedly even stealing slaves at times. If the mood struck, gang members might burn the homes of their victims, and they weren't shy about killing anyone who got in their way.

According to legend, gang members eventually accumulated $30,000 in gold, which Gale reportedly hid in Mississippi's Catahoula Swamp.

In May 1848, gang member Allen Brown got into a dispute with James Andrew Harvey of Perry County—which is now Forrest County, Mississippi—to whom Brown had sold property in exchange for a forty-dollar note. Harvey soon discovered Brown didn't have a clear title to the land and refused to pay his outstanding debt. Brown gave the note to his son-in-law, Gale, and told him he could keep the money if he collected it from Harvey. Otherwise, Wages should kill Harvey.

At the time, Gale had a baby at home. His son, Jacob Argelius Wages, was born in 1846 or early 1847. Still, Wages and Preacher McGrath saddled up and headed to Harvey's home on Red Creek. When they arrived, Wages demanded forty dollars from Harvey, who refused. According to one newspaper account at the time, Wages gave Harvey one night to come up with the money, promising to return the next night and kill him if he didn't pay. The next night, Harvey was ready with two armed relatives at his side. After either Wages or McGrath fired on Harvey, the three men opened fire, killing both Wages and McGrath.

Authorities at the time ruled that the shooting was justifiable homicide, and no charges were filed. But if another newspaper account was any indication, everyone knew Harvey had another kind of "justice" to fear. The reporter wrote that Harvey should be supplied with a bodyguard. Harvey wouldn't be in suspense about his fate for long.

Upon hearing the news of his mentor's death, James Copeland was outraged. Old Man Wages, who had always provided shelter for the outlaw gang, wanted his son's death avenged and offered a $1,000 bounty on Harvey's head. Copeland and a few gang members left for Red Creek on July 8. Their mission was successful: Harvey was shot dead. However, his murder would begin the unraveling of the Copeland Gang.

After Gale was killed, his widow, Nancy, and baby Jacob moved in with Betsy and Lloyd in Covington County. In 1849, Nancy took James H. Dannelly as her second husband, and they had seven children.

After the death of their son, Jacob and Susannah sold their Mobile farm and moved to Covington to be near Betsy's family.

CHAPTER 10

JAMES COPELAND AND THE INFAMOUS HARVEY BATTLE

In July 1848, James Copeland, by then one of the most infamous outlaws in Mississippi and Alabama, avenged the death of his friend and mentor Gale Wages by shooting to death Wages's murderer, James A. Harvey, in Mississippi.

The men in the group—Copeland and his brothers, John and Thomas, as well as Jackson Pool and Sam Stoughton—traveled from Mobile and then stopped to camp for the night near Harvey's property and made a fire to roast some corn. The smoke alerted Harvey and his men to the gang's presence, and at dawn, Harvey's men surprised the gang at its campsite. In the ensuing gun battle, Pool and Harvey were shot and killed.

Copeland and the remaining gang members fled into the woods. Copeland would remain on the run throughout the fall and into the spring of 1849.

In Copeland's posthumous biography, *Life and Confessions of the Noted Outlaw James Copeland*, recorded by Sheriff James Robert Soda Pitts, Copeland described his feelings while on the run: "I then formed a stern resolution within my own breast, that if God would permit me ever again to reach my home, that I would refrain from all my evil ways, and become a Christian, believing that God had been merciful to me, in preserving me, and hurling my comrades and associates into another world."

That spring, Copeland was arrested and indicted in Alabama for larceny and in Mississippi for Harvey's murder. While in prison, he told his life's story to Pitts, giving a detailed account of his youth and his exploits with

SECOND EDITION]   [PRICE, $1 50

LIFE AND CONFESSIONS
OF

JAMES COPELAND,
THE GREAT SOUTHERN LAND PIRATE.

THE FAMOUS HARVEY BATTLE.—[See page 183.

The cover of a book Sheriff J.R.S. Pitts
wrote about outlaw James Copeland.
Public domain.

the notorious outlaws Pitts referred to as the "Copeland and Wages Gang of Land Pirates."

James Copeland was born to Isham and Rebecca Wells Copeland near the Pascagoula River in Jackson County, Mississippi, on January 18, 1823. Isham was a fairly well-to-do farmer with slaves and plenty of livestock. Isham was determined that his children get an education and sent James to school along with his siblings. Instead, young James learned to steal small items, such as pocketknives and money, from friends. He was also known to take revenge on classmates who made him angry by lying to the teacher about a manufactured wrongdoing that would lead to the students' "flogging."

He was known as a troublemaker from an early age, yet his mother could see nothing but an angelic son. When James got into trouble, Rebecca would protect him or make excuses for his wicked ways. Copeland told Pitts that his mother "has been the principal and great cause of all my crimes and misfortunes, by stimulating me to the commission of those deeds that have brought me to what I am." In one such case, James was sent to get some greens from a neighbor, Mrs. Helverson, and borrowed a knife to cut them. Mrs. Helverson had asked James to be careful with the expensive knife and be sure to return it. Instead, he said he lost it and sneaked away with it hidden at the bottom of the bag beneath the greens.

When the knife was discovered in his possession, he claimed he had bought it in Mobile "and proved it by my mother who always upheld me in my rascality." James was making no friends in his hometown, but the turning point from troublemaker to criminal came when James was fourteen years old.

One night, he stole some of Mr. Helverson's pigs and sold them in Mobile for two dollars per head. The scheme was so simple that James got greedy and made a second attempt to steal Helverson's livestock. This time, young

James was caught and turned over to the law. Charged with larceny, he faced considerable jail time.

However, his mother once again came to his aid, sending a message to the well-known outlaw Gale Wages in Mobile, asking if he could help her son.

Wages traveled to the Copeland home in Mississippi to make plans to keep James from prison. James was taken with the older outlaw, who was at that time twenty-one years old, and the course of his life was sealed. Eventually, some of Copeland's brothers joined him, and the clan became known primarily as the Copeland Gang. James later described Wages:

> *Although a villain as I must now acknowledge Wages was, yet he had some redeeming traits in his character. At his own home he was friendly, kind and hospitable; in company, he was affable and polite; and no person at first acquaintance, would have believed for one moment that he was the out lawed [sic] brigand. I firmly believe he would have spilt the last drop of blood in his veins to protect me yet I must say that he was the principal author of my misfortunes, and has brought me where I am.*

After Wages and James burned down the courthouse at Americus, destroying arrest records and effectively wiping James's slate clean, the teenager joined Wages's gang in Mobile.

The clan, which had varying numbers and eventually topped out at sixty members, held meetings in a wigwam. Wages, as president, issued an oath to incoming members if the rest of the gang approved them. Young James took the oath with his hand on a Bible:

> *You solemnly swear upon the Holy Evangelist of Almighty God, that you will never divulge, and always conceal and never reveal any of the signs or pass-words of our order; that you will not invent any sign, token or device by which the secret mysteries of our order may be made known; that you will not in any way betray or cause to be betrayed any member of this order—the whole under pain of having your head severed from your body—so help you God.*

Then young Copeland was required to memorize a variety of signs and passwords, as well as a special alphabet invented by the Murrell gang of Tennessee that was used to send messages.

Sheriff Pitts, who later became Copeland's biographer, said the period was a perfect time for the gang to commit "daring robberies and wholesale

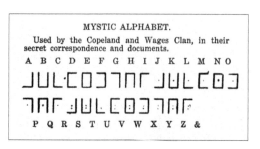

MYSTIC ALPHABET.

Used by the Copeland and Wages Clan, in their secret correspondence and documents.

A B C D E F G H I J K L M N O

P Q R S T U V W X Y Z &

Secret alphabet used by the Copeland-Wages gang. *From* Life and Confessions of the Noted Outlaw James Copeland, *public domain.*

murders," as it was a time when people carried their money on them and traveled in easily accessible carriages and stagecoaches.

Gang members plundered and rioted at will, including one night when they burned much of Mobile's business district, with gang members wearing "false moustaches and false whiskers...and many dressed like sailors ready for action with false keys, lock picks and crow bars. Each man had a revolver and Bowie knife."

The gang's haul that night was estimated at a total of $25,000, including $5,000 in jewelry and $3,000 in clothing, as well as groceries and liquors. Then the pillagers set fire to each store and loaded two large boats they had taken to Dog River.

At times, the gang would travel to other towns, and Wages's second-in-command, Charles "Preacher" McGrath, would pose as a pastor "being an Irishman and his tongue tipped with plenty of blarney." He would host a rowdy revival, luring unsuspecting townspeople away from homes and businesses. Other gang members were then free to loot at will. But Copeland had his doubts about McGrath, whom he described as "wanting in stability; that he was too wild and uncertain in his actions."

Copeland, though, was equally brutal, telling Pitts: "I believed in never leaving any living witnesses behind to tell what I had done if there was any way to prevent it."

Nothing was off limits for gang members, who simply took what they wanted, including people. They would often steal slaves and sell them. Copeland recalled a time when he took a mulatto slave from a home he had robbed, promising the girl he would marry her and free her. He lived with her for a while before selling her for $1,000. He later told Pitts: "I must here acknowledge that my conscience did that time feel mortified, after the girl had come with me, and I had lived with her as a wife, and she had such implicit confidence in me. My conscience still feels mortified when I reflect how much better it would have been for me to have kept her and lived with her than to come to what I have."

Despite his later twinge of conscience, Copeland helped Wages and McGrath amass a fortune of more than $30,000: "I then proposed to Wages

Drawing of James Copeland.
Wikimedia Commons.

and McGrath to make the amount in gold, thirty thousand dollars even, and bury it in some safe place, secure, so that we might have it for any emergency; and in case of the death of one of us, the other two were to share it; and if two died, one had all."

The men put $10,000 each in "three strong kegs" and buried them in a swamp on Hamilton Creek near Mobile. But the gang was changing. In 1843, Gale Wages began courting the daughter of gang member Allen Brown, a man who would soon become a burden to Wages, and married her in December 1845. During the intervening months, two big events occurred in the gang, which had grown to an unwieldy and nearly unmanageable number. Wages killed seven members accused as "spies and traitors," and he entered the business of printing counterfeit money. Sometime after the gang members were killed, Wages, Copeland and McGrath moved the kegs of gold to Catahoula Swamp in Hancock County, Mississippi.

The counterfeiting operation made Copeland nervous. It was Wages's father-in-law, Allen Brown, who lured him into printing money. Copeland felt Brown was a burden to Wages, who spent much of his money feeding and clothing Brown and his gang.

Eventually, Wages's association with Brown and his scam of James Harvey would be his downfall and the death knell for the gang.

"And that same pitiful note, and Brown's rascality and falsehood cost Wages and McGrath their lives, and Harvey and Pool their lives, and have placed me where I am," Copeland later told Sheriff J.R.S. Pitts while dictating his memoir. Brown was "nearly broke," so his son-in-law bought Harvey's note from him and loaned him sixty dollars, as well. Brown told Wages to get the money Harvey owed or to kill him. Instead, Harvey shot and killed Wages and McGrath.

"This news sounded in my ears like thunder, and so astonished was I that I lost for the time all my senses. Almost instantly it seemed that every crime that I had ever committed in my life was then pictured before my eyes and the awful consequences attending them," Copeland said.

Grief stricken, Gale's parents, Jacob and Susannah Wages, sought vengeance, telling Copeland: "James, we will give you one thousand dollars for Harvey's scalp, if you will kill that rascal or have it done."

So Copeland set out on July 8, 1848, with his brothers and Pool and Stoughton for Harvey's home in Mississippi. Harvey was killed in the ensuing gun battle, but Copeland was forced into hiding and didn't like living on the lam. He was arrested in the spring of 1849 and served four years in prison in Wetumpka, Alabama, after pleading guilty on the Alabama charges to avoid going to trial in Mississippi.

But Pitts, the twenty-one-year-old sheriff of Perry County, Mississippi, where the shootout occurred, transferred Copeland to jail there. Two years later, Copeland went to trial for Harvey's murder and was convicted. Copeland remained jailed during an appeal, but by 1857, his time had run out.

The death warrant said Copeland was sentenced to be "hanged by the neck until he be dead on the 30th day of October in the year of our Lord, one thousand eight hundred and fifty seven, between the hours of ten o'clock a.m. and four o'clock p.m. at the place appointed by law."

Before his death, Copeland wrote a self-pitying letter to his mother, dated October 29, 1857, from Augusta, Mississippi:

Mrs. Rebecca Copeland:

My dear Mother—It is with painful feelings indeed that I attempt writing to you on the present occasion. I take this opportunity, knowing at the same time, that it is the last one of the kind which I shall ever be permitted to enjoy while here on earth. It is long and much that I have suffered while in prison since my first conferment in Mobile county, and yet it seems as though nothing will pay the debt but my life. I have had my trial and was convicted upon a charge of murder, and I have received the awful sentence of death. The sheriff told me to-day, that to-morrow at 2 o'clock I will be hanged, according to the order of the court. Oh, my dear mother, what an awful sound is this to reach your ear. Oh, would it could be otherwise; but you are aware that I justly merit the sentence. You are knowing to my being a bad man; and dear mother, had you given me the proper advice when young, I would not perhaps be doing well. It is often I have meditated on this subject since my confinement in prison, and often have I recollected my good old father's advice when I was young, and repented a thousand times over, with sorrow and regret, that I have failed to receive it as good, benevolent advice. If such a course I had taken, I have no doubt, but I would be doing well at this time. But it is too late now to talk of things past and gone. The time has come when I shall have to take my departure from this world, and it pains my heart, to know that I have to leave you and my brothers and sisters; and much am I mortified to think how distantly you have treated me while here in prison. Not the first time have you been to see me; but I can freely excuse you for all this, and I do hope you will prepare to meet Jesus in Heaven.

Dear Mother, long has the time been that life was not any satisfaction to me. I am now in the dungeon with the cold and icy bands clasped around me, and cold as clay. Much have I suffered, but after 2 o'clock tomorrow, my trouble will all be over or worse than they are at present. This I am not able to tell. I have been preparing to meet my God, praying diligently for mercy and for the pardon of my sins, but I do not know whether my prayers have been heard or not. The Scriptures say "that the spirit of the Lord shall not always strive with man," and I again say: "He that calls upon the Lord in the last hours shall be saved." If so, I feel some spark of hope, but I tell you this hope is hanging upon a slender thread.

Dear Mother, it makes the tears trickle down my cold cheeks to have to pen this statement to you.

Dear Mother, I have to close this letter. My heart is overflowed already, so when you receive this you can keep it as a memorial and remember that poor Jim is no more on earth; that he has bid you a long farewell.

Dear Mother, it appears as though my heart will break at the very thought of this. Oh, could I but see you once more before my death, it would give my aching heart some relief; but we have to part without this pleasure. Now my good old Mother, I bid you a long farewell, forever and forever.

—James Copeland

A wooden gallows was erected outside the jail. Pitts, who had spent the intervening years recording Copeland's memories, was to act as executioner. The day was beautiful, typical of a fall day in the Deep South. Pitts wrote, "The sky was blue and serene, all nature was clam and peaceful."

The sheriff estimated ten thousand spectators attended. Copeland addressed the crowd. "He especially urged the young men present to take warning from his career and fate and to avoid bad company," Pitts wrote.

With his hands tied and a hood pulled over his head, Copeland uttered: "Lord have mercy on me!"

Copeland was praying when the trapdoor fell and his neck was broken.

No one came to claim Copeland's body, so he was buried in a steep bank, but his body disappeared after a few days, Pitts wrote.

A legend arose that a skeleton on display in a drugstore in Hattiesburg was Copeland's remains, strung with wire. The gruesome artifact "finally disappeared and has never been seen again," Pitts wrote.

J.R.S. Pitts published his account of Copeland's memories of the gang's "perfect reign of terror" in the 1858 book *Life and Confessions of the Noted Outlaw James Copeland: Executed at Augusta, Perry County, Mississippi; Leader of the Notorious Copeland and Wages Clan Which Terrorized the Entire Southern States, Related by Himself in Prison after He Was Condemned to Death, Giving a List of All Members of the Clan.*

In a "Sketch of the Author" in the front of an edition of the book released in 1909, Pitts was described as "courageous" for acting as Copeland's jailer when, at any moment, members of the brutal gang might attempt to free him: "Few sheriffs ever served through such trying times, for during the entire time after Copeland became a prisoner under him there, there was not an hour that his life was not in danger and not a day that there was not a risk to be taken in the discharge of some duty which only a brave, courageous, conscientious officer would have dared to perform."

The introduction says the sale of the book was "progressing wonderfully" until Pitts was sued in Mobile for libel because of the people named in the book.

However, Pitts had signed certificates from witnesses saying they heard Copeland give Pitts permission to reveal his story, including this one from T.C. Carter of Mobile, who wrote, "This is to certify that I was present at the execution of James Copeland, who was executed in Augusta, Perry County, Miss., the 30th day of October, 1857; and heard the Sheriff, JRS Pitts, ask him, the said James Copeland, if the detailed history and list of names given as members of the Wages and Copeland clan were correct, and he answered the Sheriff in the affirmative that they were."

Pitts eventually won his case and, in the rerelease of the book, gave an account of the trial justifying publication of the book.

With the gang disbanded, Pitts hung up his sheriff's badge, went to medical college and became a physician and later served as a Mississippi legislator, postmaster and county superintendent. He died on December 22, 1920, at the age of eighty-eight.

CHAPTER 11

FRANK AND JESSE JAMES

ACCUSED IN ALABAMA

When someone mentions outlaws, many times images of the old West come to mind, and more often than not, the name Jesse James will soon follow. His exploits and larger-than-life legend ingrained him as part of American culture.

Jesse James was the younger brother of Alexander Franklin James, who history remembers as Frank James. The brothers, born in Missouri, committed crimes in numerous states, and they eventually left their marks on Alabama. They earned their reputations as outlaws separately, together and as part of the notorious James-Younger Gang, but not until after they served in the Civil War.

The atrocities they observed and took part in during the war did much to shape the future of the two notorious outlaws. The older Frank joined the Missouri State Guard and fought to push the Union out of Missouri but was unsuccessful. During the Siege of Lexington, Missouri, Frank fell ill and was captured by Union forces. He was soon paroled and returned home to Missouri, where he was captured by local Unionists and forced to sign an allegiance to the Union, which he despised.

On August 21, 1863, Union militiamen attacked the farm belonging to Frank and Jesse's stepfather, looking for Southern conspirators. In the end, more than two hundred civilians were killed, leading Frank and Jesse to join a Confederate militia known as Quantrill's Raiders. When the Confederate army was finally driven from the state in 1864, Quantrill's Raiders was one of the many groups known as "bushwhackers" that harassed the Union army in the state.

Jesse James. *Wikimedia Commons.*

The James-Younger Gang originated as a group of Confederate bushwhackers who fought in the bitter partisan conflict that divided the state of Missouri during the Civil War. This group's postwar crimes began in 1866, though they did not truly become the James-Younger Gang until 1868, when the authorities first named Cole Younger and both the James brothers as suspects in the robbery of the Nimrod Long Bank in Russellville, Kentucky.

Membership in the gang fluctuated from robbery to robbery, as the outlaws' raids were often separated by many months. At various times, it included the Younger brothers—Cole, John, Bob and Jim—Frank James, Jesse James, Clell Miller, Arthur McCoy, Charlie Pitts, John Jarrette, Bill Chadwell (also known as Bill Stiles) and Matthew "Ace" Nelson. Some

This building, which has since been torn down, was once the Madison County jail, where Frank James was held during his Huntsville, Alabama trial. *Authors' collection.*

people theorized that the Younger brothers and the James brothers were related, but no proof exists that the groups were related by blood.

Many robberies, thefts, shootouts and other crimes have been attributed to the James brothers even though many of the crimes were actually committed by other outlaws, but the Jameses' reputations made them easy targets for blame.

The James brothers' time in Alabama has widely been seen as the beginning of the end for the infamous outlaws. In Huntsville, Alabama, legend says that Jesse James robbed the First National Bank of $10,000 at two o'clock in the afternoon on September 7, 1876. This robbery was never committed or even attempted, but the legend persists.

The closest Jesse James ever came to robbing a bank in Huntsville was when he robbed the Huntington Bank in Huntington, Tennessee, on September 15, 1875. At about noon, the outlaw, accompanied by Cole Younger and two members of his gang, leisurely entered the bank and took $10,252 from the cashier at gunpoint. The bandits were pursued by the local sheriff. James and Younger were able to escape, but the other gang members were rounded up by a sheriff's posse.

While Jesse did not rob any banks in the state of Alabama, he is rumored to have hidden out in various locations in the northern part of

According to legend, in 1876, Jesse James robbed the National Bank of Huntsville, which was erected in 1835 and still stands on the downtown square. However, there is no evidence to support the claim. Frank James later stood trial in Huntsville for another crime. *Authors' collection.*

The historical marker for the National Bank of Huntsville building. *Authors' collection.*

the state. Some of the most rumored hideout locations were near Gadsden in Etowah County, near Guntersville in Marshall County and Mentone in DeKalb County.

Elder brother Frank also never robbed a bank in Huntsville, but he came a lot closer than Jesse did—at least according to the state's judicial system.

On March 11, 1881, a federal paymaster by the name of Alexander G. Smith was traveling from Florence to Muscle Shoals, Alabama, transporting the payroll for the men digging a canal in Muscle Shoals for the U.S. Army Corps of Engineers. This payroll consisted of $4,371 in cash, $500 in gold and $419.18 in silver. Smith rode on horseback, and three men rode up beside him and asked for directions to a local creek. After Smith described the route, the men rode off in the direction of the creek while Smith continued his journey to Muscle Shoals.

A few miles up the road, Smith again saw the men, who were by now wearing masks and pointing revolvers at the lone paymaster. Two of the men dismounted and approached Smith, taking his gun from him. The two outlaws then took the payroll bag, as well as fifty dollars in cash, from the terrified Smith. One of the outlaws asked Smith if the fifty dollars were his or belonged to the government. When Smith replied that it was his personal money, the outlaws gave the money back to him. The outlaws then forced Smith at gunpoint to ride with them for several miles before releasing him.

The three robbers rode into the woods, where they split the money and then went their separate ways. One of the men who split the money that afternoon soon made his way to the tiny town of White's Creek just north of Nashville, Tennessee, where the unraveling of the James gang would begin. The man's name was Bill Ryan, and like so many others before and after him, he had a problem keeping his mouth shut once he had a few drinks.

While in a bar in the small town, Ryan was drinking whiskey and bragging about being an "outlaw against state, county, and the United States Government." One of the bar patrons tired of Ryan's bragging and began to question the outlaw. Ryan became outraged and, in his drunken state, drew his guns to demand an apology. Luck was not on his side that night, and instead of receiving his apology, Ryan was wrestled to the ground and subdued by the bartender, who happened to be an off-duty deputy sheriff.

Ryan was arrested and taken to jail in Nashville, where lawmen discovered a large amount of money and gold in his possession. Authorities began to question where he obtained the money and soon coaxed the tale of the Muscle Shoals army payroll robbery from Ryan. Soon, Frank and Jesse James were implicated in the robbery.

In early 1882, Jesse had become paranoid and moved back to Missouri, where he felt more at ease. He made a deal with local outlaws Charley and Bob Ford to move in with them and their families in St. Joseph for added protection. On the morning of April 3, 1882, Jesse and the Ford brothers were preparing to leave for another robbery. The warm morning saw the group going in and out of the house preparing their horses and supplies for the upcoming crime. Because he was at home, Jesse was not wearing his usual revolver. On one of the trips into the house, Jesse stopped to dust a picture, when Bob Ford approached the outlaw from behind, fired one shot into the back of his head and ended the life of one of history's most famous outlaws.

The Ford brothers made no attempt to hide the murder, and Bob petitioned the governor for the $5,000 reward that had been placed on James. The brothers were therefore dismayed when they were charged with murder. In the course of a single day, the Ford brothers were indicted, pleaded guilty and sentenced to death by hanging, and two hours later, they were granted a full pardon by Governor Thomas Crittenden. Details later emerged that Bob Ford had been in secret negotiations with the governor to capture James. The governor's quick pardon suggested he knew the brothers intended to kill James rather than capture him. The implication that the chief executive of Missouri conspired to kill a private citizen startled the public and added to James's notoriety. The outlaw's death caused such a stir that throngs of people visited Jesse's house to see his body. The Ford brothers would later star in a traveling stage show where they reenacted James's execution.

Jesse's murder struck his family hard. Jesse's mother, Zerelda Samuel, was so grief-stricken by his death she wrote this epitaph:

In Loving Memory of my Beloved Son, Murdered by a Traitor and Coward Whose Name is not Worthy to Appear Here.

A few months after the shooting, on October 4, 1882, Frank James went to Jefferson City, Missouri, for an appointment with Governor Crittenden. During this meeting, Frank handed his holstered gun over to the governor and told him: "I have been hunted for twenty-one years, have literally lived in the saddle, have never known a day of perfect peace. It was one long, anxious, inexorable, eternal vigil." He then ended his statement by saying, "Governor, I haven't let another man touch my gun since 1861."

It has been said that Frank surrendered to the governor with the understanding that he would never be extradited to Minnesota to face several charges in that state.

This historical marker in downtown Huntsville, Alabama, is near the spot where Frank James's trial was held. *Authors' collection.*

He was never sent to Minnesota, but he was indicted on various robbery and murder charges in Gallatin, Missouri, and for the July 15, 1881 robbery of the Rock Island train at Winston, Missouri, in which the train's engineer and a passenger were killed. He was exonerated after prosecutors were unable to provide enough evidence of his involvement. After his acquittal in Gallatin, he was then taken to Huntsville, Alabama, to stand trial for the Muscle Shoals U.S. Army Corps of Engineers payroll robbery.

Frank James arrived in Huntsville in March 1884 at a time when the country was enamored of the legend of the James brothers. An entire entertainment industry had been built around their adventures. Dime stores across America carried pulp novels and magazines that thrilled their readers with the gang's exploits.

While in Huntsville awaiting trial, Frank was incarcerated in the Madison County jail, but he was far from an average prisoner. During his stay, he was almost a tourist attraction, and people came from miles around to see the famous outlaw. Certain people of Huntsville society were given special access to Frank James and were able to sign him out of the jail for a few hours at a time. Once, Huntsville attorney William Hundley was allowed to take Frank from jail to go quail hunting.

Even though he was treated with celebrity status in jail, Frank missed his wife, from whom he had been separated for many months. Shortly after his arrival he wrote her a letter from the jail dated March 26, 1884, in which he says he's anticipating a visit.

> *My Darling Wife.*
>
> *Yours of the 21ˢᵗ rec'd I anticipated your movements and addressed my letter of yesterday to Independence. Do you know I consider this last letter of yours decidedly the best effort of your life. It was to the point and remember, I will certainly treasure it up as I would some rare gem, I was very much impressed with the idea that you and Rob were delighted with the idea of coming to see me. Time will drag until your arrival, what do you think William H. Wallace is in Nashville there acting in conjunction with one Bradshaw, a detective from Kansas City who has been there several days. Well, all he finds out I think he will be able to note on his thumbnail, I had expected as much and posted Glover to be on the lookout, I suppose he will follow me to the end. Let him he will meet fervor worthy of his still. We will be fully prepared never fear about that. By the time you get this you will be ready to start, if trains are not running through to Memphis. You can come the other route. I would suggest that you buy your ticket at Kansas City through to Nashville in the event you have to come that way, I expect you can get it cheaper than from Independence, you can go into Mr. Wrights and telephone to the agent in Kansas City and find out. I want you to get here as soon as you come [sic] no matter which route you come. Be sure to remember me to all my friends, so good bye darling, I am*
>
>

Your loving husband

Frank James

>
> *Tell Mr. Glover that Wallace is on deck and is still crying for my blood, The contemptible dog, and that he is, I hope to live to see the day to tell what I think.*

Newspaper reporters from far and wide descended on what was then the small town of Huntsville, filled its hotels and boardinghouses and filed sensational reports on the latest developments in the case. Huntsville, for a time, became a city on the national stage. This exposure added to the anticipation of the trial, which began on April 17, 1884.

On the day of the trial, Frank entered the courtroom accompanied by his wife, young son and an all-star legal team headed by veteran Huntsville

Left: Leroy Pope Walker. *Madison County Historical Society*.

Right: Frank James. *Wikimedia Commons*.

lawyer Leroy Pope Walker, who had been the secretary of war for the Confederacy. The prosecution was led by William H. Smith, U.S. attorney and former governor of Alabama.

It did not take long for the reporters in the courtroom to realize they were in the right place for juicy material as the two attorneys sparred and jousted in front of a jury made up largely of Civil War veterans. Leroy Pope Walker understood his jury and emphasized in his opening statement that Frank had also fought for the Southern cause, having served with the Missouri irregulars under William Clarke Quantrill during the closing days of the war. Smith, for his part, countered with the facts of the case. He brought out witnesses who identified Frank as one of the robbers, but under cross-examination, Walker got each to recant his claims. After a parade of witnesses by the defense who swore that they saw Frank in Nashville on the day of the robbery and a brilliant final summation by Leroy Pope Walker, the jury reached its verdict: Frank James was acquitted of all charges against him.

He walked out of the Madison County courtroom a free man, but that did not last long. Before he could leave town, he was arrested for a July 7, 1876 robbery in Rocky Cut, Missouri. Soon after, Governor Crittenden pardoned him for that crime, and Frank's trials ended for good.

Frank James spent the next thirty years doing various jobs. He was a shoe salesman, a ticket-taker at a theater and a telegraph operator. Near the end of his life, he supported himself and his family by giving tours of the James farm in Missouri for twenty-five cents. He died at his boyhood home on February 18, 1915, at age seventy-one, leaving behind his wife and son and still celebrating his legacy as one of the most famous outlaws in history.

CHAPTER 12

ALBERT PARSONS

TERRORIST OR WORKINGMAN'S HERO?

The decades following the Civil War brought many changes throughout the United States. Slaves had been freed, Reconstruction was enacted in the South and the Industrial Revolution was beginning to change the face of America's workforce. These changes created a time during which citizens began to question democracy and capitalism in our newly re-formed country.

No one person was more at the forefront of these changes than a boy from Alabama who would grow up to be linked to one of the largest acts of domestic terrorism the country had seen to that time. He has been vilified in America's third-largest city, Chicago, for more than 125 years. Yet this man was responsible for something that most every American is familiar with—the eight-hour workday. That man is Albert Richard Parsons.

Parsons was born in June 1848—some records show his birthdate as June 20 and some as June 24—as the youngest of ten children born to Samuel and Elizabeth Parsons of Montgomery, Alabama. Samuel was a leather smith and shoemaker originally from the state of Maine.

Albert Parsons. *Wikimedia Commons.*

As an adult, Parsons claimed that his ancestors were early American pioneers who arrived at Narragansett Bay in what would later become the state of Rhode Island. He also claimed that one of his relatives on his mother's side, a Tompkins, served with George Washington during the American Revolution. On his father's side, he was descended from Major General Samuel Holden Parsons, who made a name for himself during the American Revolution.

By the time Albert was five years old, both his parents had died from illness—his mother before he was two years old and his father three years later. He was left in the care of a local slave named Esther until he was sent to live with one of his older brothers in Texas. William Henry Parsons was married and ran the *Tyler Telegraph*, a small newspaper in the town of Tyler.

In 1859, eleven-year-old Albert left his brother's house to go and live with one of his sisters in Waco, Texas. There, he attended school for a couple years before becoming an apprentice at the *Galveston Daily News*. This is where a lifelong career in journalism began.

When the Civil War began in 1861, Parsons's thirst for adventure led him to join the Confederate forces against the wishes of his family and his boss at the paper. He joined a unit known as the Lone Star Greys before enlisting in the regular Confederate army and being assigned to an artillery unit at Sabine Pass, Texas, where one of his brothers was captain of an infantry company. In this unit, the thirteen-year-old served as a "powder monkey," fetching the powder to load the cannons.

After a year of service in the artillery, Albert transferred to his brother William's unit, the Twelfth Regiment of the Texas Cavalry, also known as Parsons's Mounted Volunteers. Young Albert served as a scout in the unit that was primarily tasked with raiding along the west side of the Mississippi River in southeast Arkansas and northeast Louisiana. Federal troops referred to the Twelfth as the "Swamp Fox Regiment," because the men traveled the swamps at night and often attacked Federal positions after dark. Albert served in three campaigns with the Twelfth before the war was finished.

After the war, Albert returned to Waco, where he purchased forty acres of corn and hired recently freed slaves to help harvest the crop. He used his earnings to pay for six months' tuition at Waco University, which later became known as Baylor. That six months was about half of all the education he ever received and would account for all of his higher education.

When the college funds ran out, Albert left school and took a job in a printing office to learn the business before starting his own newspaper. In 1868, at the age of twenty, he launched the *Waco Spectator*, which championed the rights of freed slaves and encouraged people to accept the terms of the South's surrender and other Reconstruction measures. These views were unpopular in the recently defeated southern state, and his newspaper suffered for it, lasting less than a year.

Parsons then took a job as a traveling correspondent and business agent for the *Houston Daily Telegraph*, at the time one of the largest papers in Texas. During his travels, he met Lucy Ella Gonzales and began a romance.

In 1870, Parsons was appointed assistant assessor for the U.S. Internal Revenue Service, which was formed to raise funds to pay for the war, and served in that capacity until he accepted the position of chief deputy collector in Austin, Texas. He held this position until 1873, when he left Texas to relocate in Chicago.

In 1872, Parsons and Ella had wed, but the happy occasion presented a few problems for the couple. Ella was a mixed-race woman whose father was Creek Indian and whose mother was Mexican. Parsons was white, and mixed-race marriages in Texas at the time were considered socially unacceptable. It was not long before the couple drew the attention of the Ku Klux Klan, and fearing for their safety, they decided to leave Texas when Parsons secured a job as a print setter and reporter for the *Chicago Times*.

Not long after settling in the Windy City, Parsons became interested in labor politics and, along with his wife, joined the Socialist Democratic Party, which would become the Socialist Labor Party in 1876. The couple was also instrumental in establishing the International Working Men's Association, or IWMA, after the National Labor Union folded. The IWMA supported racial and gender equality among workers.

In 1876, Parsons was nominated to run for the position of Chicago city alderman by the IWMA, and despite the group's lack of political power at the time, he was able to garner one-sixth of the city's votes. Parsons ran twice more for Chicago city alderman, twice for clerk of Cook County and once for U.S. Congress, but he was never elected. These failures led him to withdraw from participation in elected politics.

In his memoir, Parsons recalled his decision to leave organized politics:

> *I withdrew from all active participation in the political Labor Party, having been convinced that the number of hours per day that the wage-workers are compelled to work, together with the low wages they received, amounted to their practical disfranchisement as voters. My experience in the Labor Party had also taught me that bribery, intimidation, duplicity, corruption, and bulldozing grew out of the conditions which made the working people*

poor and the idlers rich, and that consequently the ballot-box could not be made an index to record the popular will until the existing debasing, impoverishing, and enslaving industrial conditions were first altered.

Parsons began to spend more time focusing on the growing movement to establish the eight-hour workday. In 1880, Parsons helped launch a national lobbying movement aimed at coordinating various labor organizations to enforce the eight-hour workday.

Though he was no longer involved in politics, Parsons continued to be active in the Socialist Labor Party, and when the party was on the decline in 1881, he helped form the group into the new International Revolutionary Socialists, which would then again re-form as the International Working People's Association (WPA) in 1883. This would be the final party Parsons would align himself with.

With his new association, Parsons in 1884 launched yet another newspaper. The *Alarm* was a weekly Chicago newspaper that touted itself as "A Socialistic Weekly Publication" on its masthead, yet the publication presented unmistakable anarchist content.

His support of the eight-hour day finally began paying off, and on May 1, 1886, workers across the United States began a strike to support it. Within several more days, more than 340,000 workers, including 85,000 from the Chicago area, joined the strike, shutting down numerous industries. In Chicago, an estimated 45,000 workers were immediately granted the eight-hour day.

May 3, 1886, saw an organized protest outside the McCormick Harvester Works, where more than 1,400 laborers were on strike. This group was joined by 6,000 lumber workers, who were also striking. During a speech by IWPA leader August Spies, Chicago police officers arrived and opened fire on the crowd, resulting in the deaths of four workers.

The next day, August Spies published in his local paper, the *Arbeiter-Zeitung*, a pamphlet titled *Revenge! Workingmen to Arms!* The pamphlet, published in English and German, spoke of the previous night's bloodshed and encouraged men to rise up against the authorities. He also published a second pamphlet encouraging workers to gather for a mass protest at Haymarket Square later that evening.

More than three thousand people turned up at 10:00 p.m. at Haymarket Square. Parsons initially declined to speak, fearing violence could result. Speeches were made by August Spies and Samuel Fielden of the IWPA, which encouraged Parsons to speak. Once he completed his speech, Parsons

Left: Etching of Albert Parsons. *Wikimedia Commons.*

Below: A marker giving the history of the Haymarket Tragedy. *Historical Marker Database.*

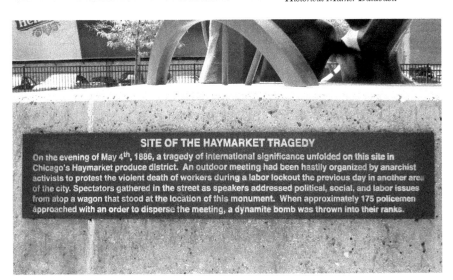

SITE OF THE HAYMARKET TRAGEDY

On the evening of May 4th, 1886, a tragedy of international significance unfolded on this site in Chicago's Haymarket produce district. An outdoor meeting had been hastily organized by anarchist activists to protest the violent death of workers during a labor lockout the previous day in another area of the city. Spectators gathered in the street as speakers addressed political, social, and labor issues from atop a wagon that stood at the location of this monument. When approximately 175 policemen approached with an order to disperse the meeting, a dynamite bomb was thrown into their ranks.

took his family and went to a local eatery, joined by several protesters. They left a large crowd at Haymarket Square that many witnesses say was peacefully dispersing when Chicago police officers arrived on the scene. Suddenly, a bomb was tossed into the square. The ensuing explosion killed one police officer and wounded several others. Police responded by firing into the crowd. A minimum of seven people died—police never confirmed an official count—and more than two hundred were injured. Most accounts placed responsibility for the injuries on police and not the bomb.

Immediately after the incident, witnesses identified Rudolph Schnaubelt as the man who threw the bomb into the crowd. Police apprehended Schnaubelt the next day, but he was later released without being charged. Numerous claims said Schnaubelt was hired by Chicago authorities to incite the event, but that has never been proven.

In the days after the Haymarket Square incident, authorities arrested Samuel Fielden, George Engel, August Spies, Adolph Fisher, Louis Lingg, Oscar Neebe and Michael Schwab, all of whom had been present at Haymarket Square. Parsons had taken his family and fled to Wisconsin after being tipped off about his pending arrest. But when the trial for the accused men was set, Parsons turned himself in to Chicago authorities to stand by his fellow IWPA members.

Several witnesses revealed that none of the men on trial threw the bomb into Haymarket Square that night, so the prosecution, headed by Julius Grinnell, instead charged the eight men with conspiracy to commit murder. The prosecutor said the men had made speeches and published articles that encouraged the unknown bomber to commit his deed. The prosecution also produced a Pinkerton Agency detective who had supposedly been working undercover to collect evidence against the men that further pointed to their acts as inflammatory. As if these allegations were not enough, jurors were allowed to read publications and speeches by the men that advocated using violence to accomplish their goals.

On August 10, 1886, the eight men were found guilty of conspiracy to commit murder. August Spies, Adolph Fisher, Louis Lingg, George Engel, Samuel Fielden, Michael Schwab and Albert Parsons were sentenced to death, while Oscar Neebe was sentenced to fifteen years in prison. Fielden and Schwab asked for clemency, and Governor Richard J. Oglesby commuted their sentences to life in prison. Parsons was also given the opportunity to ask for clemency but refused to do so, saying that asking for clemency would be an admission of guilt. Instead, Parsons seemed defiant until the very end, even in the last letter to his wife written before his execution:

Poster of the Chicago Seven.
Wikimedia Commons.

Cook County Bastille, Cell No. 29,
Chicago, August 20, 1886.
My Darling Wife:
Our verdict this morning cheers the hearts of tyrants throughout the world,
and the result will be celebrated by King Capital in its drunken feast of
flowing wine from Chicago to St. Petersburg. Nevertheless, our doom to
death is the handwriting on the wall, foretelling the downfall of hate,
malice, hypocrisy, judicial murder, oppression, and the domination of man
over his fellowman. The oppressed of earth are writhing in their legal
chains. The giant Labor is awakening. The masses, aroused from their
stupor, will snap their petty chains like reeds in the whirlwind.

We are all creatures of circumstance; we are what we have been made to
be. This truth is becoming clearer day by day.

There was no evidence that any one of the eight doomed men knew of,
or advised, or abetted the Haymarket tragedy. But what does that matter?

The privileged class demands a victim, and we are offered a sacrifice to appease the hungry yells of an infuriated mob of millionaires who will be contented with nothing less than our lives. Monopoly triumphs! Labor in chains ascends the scaffold for having dared to cry out for liberty and right!

Well, my poor, dear wife, I, personally, feel sorry for you and the helpless little babes of our loins.

You I bequeath to the people, a woman of the people. I have one request to make of you: Commit no rash act to yourself when I am gone, but take up the great cause of Socialism where I am compelled to lay it down.

My children—well, their father had better die in the endeavor to secure their liberty and happiness than live contented in a society which condemns nine-tenths of its children to a life of wage-slavery and poverty. Bless them; I love them unspeakably, my poor helpless little ones.

Ah, wife, living or dead, we are as one. For you my affection is everlasting. For the people, humanity. I cry out again and again in the doomed victim's cell: Liberty! Justice! Equality!
Albert R. Parsons.

On November 10, 1887, the night before his scheduled execution, Louis Lingg committed suicide in his jail by biting a blasting cap that had been smuggled into the jail inside a cigar. His death would precede those of his co-conspirators by only a few hours.

As Parsons was in his noose, he asked to speak: "Will I be allowed to speak, oh men of America? Let me speak, Sheriff Matson. Let the voice of the people be heard. O…" Parsons never finished his statement; the sheriff had given the signal, and the trapdoor opened up under Parsons, cutting him off midsentence as he was hanged by the neck until dead.

Parsons was buried in the Waldheim Cemetery in Chicago's Forrest Park area. The old cemetery is now called Forrest Home Cemetery, and a memorial known as the Haymarket Martyrs Monument marks his grave. His wife, Lucy, is buried nearby.

CHAPTER 13

STEVE RENFROE

ALABAMA'S OUTLAW SHERIFF

The life of any outlaw could be described as complicated and a bit mysterious, but no man in Alabama history fits these descriptions more so than Steve Renfroe, to whom history has given the title "Alabama's Outlaw Sheriff."

Stephen Renfroe was born in Georgia in 1843 to J.G. and Map Renfroe. In the latter part of 1852 or the early part of 1853, the Renfroe family followed other settlers moving west to Alabama because of the fertile farmlands. The family settled in Butler County, but little else has been recorded of the Renfroe family from this time.

History seems to overlook Stephen Renfroe until 1861, when he enlisted in the Confederate army. He was assigned to the Jeff Davis Rangers of the Ninth Alabama Infantry Regiment. The Jeff Davis Rangers were made up of men from Butler County and were later renamed Company G. Renfroe went on to serve for the majority of the war with the Ninth Alabama Infantry.

The Ninth Alabama was involved in many battles during Renfroe's service. Some of the major engagements the regiment saw were the Battle of Seven Pines, the Battle of Williamsburg, the Second Battle of Bull Run, the Battle of Antietam, the Battle of Fredricksburg and the Battle of Gettysburg. Renfroe is listed as a deserter from the unit in January 1865 while he was a private, a rank he held the majority of his time in the regiment.

After Renfroe's desertion from the unit, the Ninth Alabama continued fighting the Union forces in Virginia for nine months in what is known as the Siege of Petersburg. When the Union finally broke the Confederate supply

Drawing of outlaw sheriff Steve Renfroe. *From the* Tuscaloosa News, *1874.*

line between Petersburg and Richmond, the Ninth Alabama fell back along with the rest of the Army of Northern Virginia to Appomattox Court House, where Confederate general Robert E. Lee would eventually surrender his forces to Union general Ulysses Grant.

It is the regiment's involvement in the Siege of Petersburg and the surrender at Appomattox that saved Renfroe from capture and court-martial on desertion charges. The Confederate army had other concerns. Therefore, Renfroe returned to Butler County, where he soon caught the eye of a local woman, and on September 2, 1865, Renfroe was married to Mary E. Shepherd, known to her friends as "Mollie."

The couple lived a relatively quiet life as Steve worked as a farmer for the next two years. In the summer of 1867, he became involved in a feud with his wife's brother, Dr. Thomas Mills. The feud escalated and reached its apex on July 9, 1867, when Steve Renfroe shot and killed Mills.

It is unknown if Renfroe was justified in killing Mills, but he apparently believed he was not because he left his wife and fled to nearby Lowndes County. He eventually drifted to Sumter County, where he settled in the town of Livingston and was joined shortly afterward by Mollie.

Steve and Mollie returned to a quiet life of farming for a time, but that changed when Mollie suddenly became ill with a mysterious affliction and soon died. She was buried in Bethel Cemetery in Sumterville. No one questioned that she died of natural causes, but many locals speculated it was odd that she passed away at such a young age—she was twenty-two at the time of her death.

Some argue that the reason there was little inquiry into the death of Mollie Renfroe was that her husband was known as a handsome, dashing, quality man who was cementing a reputation as an upstanding citizen.

Others argue that Renfroe had been slowly and quietly establishing himself as an influential leader in the growing faction of the Ku Klux Klan. Sumter County had become a hotbed of **KKK** activity in the late 1860s, largely due to the postwar demographics of the county. The recorded number of former slaves in the county was 18,091, while the recorded number of white residents was only 5,919, which is a more than a three-to-one margin.

Renfroe did not grieve the loss of his wife for long before he caught the eye of another Mary: nineteen-year-old Mary M. Sledge, known to the community as "Pattie." The two were married on November 11, 1869, six days before her twentieth birthday. Like Steve's previous wife, Pattie soon developed a mysterious illness, and after less than two years of marriage, the young Pattie also died. She was buried in the Old Sides Cemetery in Sumterville. Oddly, Renfroe had the body of his first wife exhumed and brought to Old Sides Cemetery, where she was reinterred alongside his second wife. Once again, no one in the community publicly raised questions regarding the young woman's death.

After Pattie's death, Renfroe continued his rise in the ranks of the **KKK**. The full extent of his involvement in the organization has never been revealed, but locals at the time felt that Renfroe was a powerful and respected force in the **KKK** who no one was interested in challenging.

Renfroe was able to charm yet another young lady in the waning months of 1872. His courtship of twenty-year-old Cherry Reynolds eventually led to their wedding on January 9, 1873, Renfroe's third marriage in eight years.

Renfroe's rising respect in the **KKK** and reputation in the community gave him confidence that he could attain public office. He ran for sheriff of Sumter County and was elected to the position in 1878. Local reports claim that it was not long after this that the new sheriff became "crooked."

Among the new sheriff's indiscretions reported by the local newspaper, the *Livingston Journal*, were "drinking on the job, blackmail, arson, thieving, twice robbing his own office, and other almost inconceivable outrages." A local lawyer and friend of Renfroe had this to say about the sheriff: "It is well established that while he was sheriff he burned the clerk's office, robbed himself of money he had collected for other people, embezzled money, used trust funds, turned prisoners out of jail, committed an unprovoked assault with intent to murder, and was guilty of various thefts."

Deeds like these could not go unnoticed for long, and in less than two years, federal marshals arrived in Sumter County and arrested Renfroe for his various crimes. He was remanded to custody in the Sumter County jail. On June 19, 1880, Renfroe made his first of many escapes from jail by cutting a hole in the wall of his cell and jumping to the roof of a nearby shed and then to the ground.

On July 19, 1880, exactly one month after his first jailbreak, Renfroe signed the deed to his home and property to his wife, Cherry, and disappeared. For the next couple years, nothing was heard from Renfroe. Many have speculated that during this time he joined the well-known Harrison Gang and spent that time committing crimes in Louisiana and Mississippi.

In the latter months of 1882, Renfroe reappeared in Sumter County with no explanation of where he had been. His wife refused to recognize him, and law enforcement officials refused to arrest the former sheriff when he tried to turn himself in. Not finding satisfaction in his former town, Renfroe once again pulled a disappearing act, this time for a year.

Renfroe returned to Sumter in the spring of 1884 and, once again, attempted to turn himself in for his past crimes. This time, the county sheriff was more than willing to accept the outlaw's surrender and take him into custody in the county jail. Renfroe would attempt another escape but without his previous success.

Because of his history of jailbreaks, Renfroe was transferred to the Tuscaloosa County jail. Someone smuggled a knife to him, and he began the slow process of once again cutting a hole in the wall of his second-floor cell, a task that took months. He escaped on July 7 after writing a note to the sheriff, pushing himself through the plaster to the bottom floor and tossing his uneaten dinner to the guard dogs to keep them occupied. Then he climbed the outside fence to freedom.

It is rumored that after the escape, Renfroe returned briefly to Sumter County before setting off for Mississippi and Louisiana, where his whereabouts were unaccounted for. It is rumored that he rode with outlaws who made raids all the way into Texas and Mexico. Lawmen caught his trail in the summer of 1885, and Renfroe was tracked to Slidell, Louisiana. He was arrested and incarcerated in New Orleans before being returned to Tuscaloosa to stand trial for his previous crimes.

The former sheriff was found guilty of multiple crimes during his trial in 1885 and was sentenced to five years in the mines at Flat Rock at the age of forty-two. This was considered to be hard labor and a harsh sentence, but as with his previous incarcerations, Renfroe would not be held for long.

On October 3, he escaped from the Tuscaloosa jail with three other prisoners. The men apparently had an auger smuggled into the jail and were able to bore through the stone walls. Once he escaped, he parted ways with the other prisoners and headed back toward Sumter County. Officials interviewed a hobo who said he met Renfroe near Eutaw in Coffee County and walked with him to Livingston, arriving in the Sumter County town on October 10, 1885. There, he made a hideout in the woods outside town.

One of the many legends surrounding the outlaw sheriff says that, as Christmas 1885 neared, Renfroe was becoming antsy alone in the woods, so he headed to Meridian, Mississippi, where he found a journalist to whom he recounted his deeds and misdeeds. The reporter promised not to tell authorities of Renfroe's whereabouts. The reporter's story was either never published or has been lost to history, or perhaps the journalist's meeting was merely a legend.

Renfroe remained hidden until the summer of 1886, when he was captured on July 11 by a group of farmers near the town of Enterprise, Mississippi. The farmers turned the outlaw over to authorities who returned him to Livingston, Alabama, on July 13. He was met by throngs of spectators calling for the former sheriff to be hanged. One man present at Renfroe's homecoming later wrote: "To hang Renfroe was determined upon by everybody without any special understanding about it."

Late that afternoon, a lynch mob consisting of eight men stormed the Livingston jail where Renfroe was being held, threatened the jailer to obtain the keys and then removed Renfroe from his cell. The men then marched the outlaw sheriff through the main street of Livingston in an almost parade-like fashion. Tempie Scruggs, who witnessed this parade from her front porch, later said: "We knew something terrible was going to happen, and we dropped down on the porch and watched them through the railing. They were so quiet."

There are two versions of Steve Renfroe's demise. The first and most popular version is that the lynch mob marched the outlaw to the Alamuchee-Bellamy covered bridge, where he was hanged from a cross beam and left hanging, blocking the roadway until the sheriff and his men came and cut down the body.

The second version of the tale is that the men marched Renfroe through town to a chinaberry tree on the banks of the Sucarnochee River not far from the covered bridge. There, the leader of the mob told Renfroe: "We are all your friends, Steve. We are doing this for your own good."

To this the former sheriff replied: "I wish one of you would say a prayer for me." The leader of the men bowed his head, saying, "Lord, please rest this miserable soul," and as he finished, Renfroe was hanged from the tree.

Whichever of these accounts is true, the Sumter County sheriff and his deputies took Steve Renfroe's body back to Livingston, but no one from his

Some legends claim Steve Renfroe was hanged on the Alamuchee-Bellamy covered bridge. *Wikimedia Commons.*

family came to claim it. Several days went by, and the outlaw sheriff was given a quiet, secret pauper's burial in an unmarked grave in a field somewhere on the outskirts of town.

No one was ever charged in the lynching of Steve Renfroe. It is reported that the jailer who gave the mob the keys knew the identity of the members of the group, but he never revealed their names. Most of the citizens of Livingston were witness to Renfroe's grisly parade through town, but none came forward with information. It is also questionable if the sheriff's office investigated the death, perhaps instead considering the event to be in the best interests of the community.

More than 120 years after the outlaw sheriff was hanged, some locals feel that his spirit has never left. Some say that his spirit roams across the old Alamuchee-Bellamy covered bridge trying in vain to get someone to notice him and satisfy his need for attention. Others will say that you can go down to the bank of the Sucarnochee River, find the ancient chinaberry tree and watch the limbs sway when there is no wind, almost as if Alabama's outlaw sheriff is still swinging from the end of his noose.

CHAPTER 14

JOHN WESLEY HARDIN'S ALABAMA YEARS

On his twenty-first birthday on May 26, 1874, notorious Texas outlaw John Wesley "Wes" Hardin committed the crime that forced him to take an alias and go into hiding for three years, eighteen months of which were spent in Alabama: he shot and killed Deputy Sheriff Charles Webb in Brown County.

Born in 1853 to a circuit-riding preacher in Texas, Hardin would kill his first of an estimated twenty-seven men when he was fifteen years old. He would spend the rest of his life pursued by the law, committing crimes or imprisoned. Newspapers of the period and Hardin's autobiography describe an encounter with lawman "Wild Bill" Hickock in Abilene, Texas, where Hardin killed a man for snoring and fled town in fear of Hickock's retribution.

Despite Hardin's bloody history, during his time in Alabama under the alias "J.H. Swain," many residents who were unaware he was a wanted criminal thought of him as a gentleman. From late 1875 until the summer of 1877, Hardin's wife, Jane, and their children lived in Pollard, Alabama, with Jane's uncles, who were both lawmen, while Hardin used Pollard as a base and traveled to Mobile and Florida swindling people out of money at cards.

Following Hardin's final capture in Florida in 1877, resident Robert Warren Brooks wrote a series of articles for the newspaper in Atmore,

Alabama, about his relationship with the outlaw, describing him as "among the politest and nicest looking men I came into contact with in my younger days...he was a fine, upstanding man with a high forehead, curly hair and deep blue eyes, and looked more like a college professor than what he turned out to be. He and I got to be really chummy...If Hardin ever carried a gun, I never saw it."

An obituary published in the August 22, 1895 edition of the *Gonzales Inquirer* described Hardin:

> *In personal appearance Hardin was as typical a Texas desperado of the earliest type as was ever portrayed in a dime novel. He was of medium weight, nearly six feet tall, straight as an arrow and dark complexioned, with an eye as keen as a hawk.*
>
> *As an expert shot he was the peer of either King Fisher or Ben Thompson in their palmiest days. He could shoot as quickly and aim as straight as either of them. It was almost sure death for anyone who was in front of his gun when Hardin drew a bead.*
>
> *Seventeen scalps are said to have dangled from his belt and it is likely that the number of human lives that he has taken will exceed that number.*

Wes Hardin was born near Bonham, Texas, on May 26, 1853, to James "Gip" and Mary Elizabeth Dixon Hardin. Gip was a Methodist preacher who named his son for John Wesley, the church's founder. The family eventually settled in Sumpter, Texas, where Gip founded a school that Wes and his nine siblings attended.

In 1862, eight-year-old Wes tried to run off and join the Confederate army but was stopped.

When he was fifteen, Hardin's life as an outlaw began with a seemingly innocuous challenge to wrestle Maje, a former slave of his uncle Holshousen. Hardin won the match, but Wes would later claim Maje ambushed him on a path the next day, forcing him to draw his revolver and fire five shots into Maje.

Hardin wrote in his autobiography, *The Life of John Wesley Hardin as Written by Himself*, that he went to get help for Maje, who died three days later. Gip Hardin, fearing his son would not receive a fair trial in the Union-occupied state, sent his son into hiding. Hardin wrote that he was discovered, and three Union soldiers came to arrest him. He chose not to go willingly.

He wrote: "I waylaid them, as I had no mercy on men whom I knew only wanted to get my body to torture and kill. It was war to the knife for me, and

I brought it on by opening the fight with a double-barrelled [*sic*] shotgun and ended it with a cap and ball six-shooter. Thus it was by the fall of 1868 I had killed four men and was myself wounded in the arm."

Neil Bowen, who would become Wes Hardin's father-in-law, was born in Escambia County, Florida, near the Alabama state line and had numerous relatives in Pollard in adjoining Escambia County, Alabama, including several lawmen.

Bowen married Mary Western in Escambia County in 1848, and the next year, Mary gave birth to a son, Robert Joshua "Brown" Bowen. Florida Nancy Bowen was born in Florida in 1850 before the family moved to Texas. The couple had four more children: Mary Elizabeth Bowen, Jane Ann Bowen, Martha Ella Bowen and Julia Ann Bowen. Two of the Bowen children, Brown and Jane, would earn places in history by their connections to Wes Hardin—Brown as a fellow outlaw and Jane as Wes's wife.

Jane's father was operating a mercantile in the town of Nopal in 1872 when Jane and Wes decided to marry. They wed in Gonzalez County, Texas, in 1872 when she was fifteen and he was eighteen.

Jane's brother Brown, who was twenty-five at the time, began riding with Hardin's gang of outlaws, which would eventually lead to his untimely demise and cause a rift between Jane and her family.

By 1874, Hardin had been accused in numerous killings, typically eluding capture, but when he was caught, he managed to escape, such as the time in 1871 when seventeen-year-old Wes escaped by shooting to death his guard, Jim Smalley.

In 1872, after being wounded by a shotgun blast during an argument over a card game in Trinity, Texas, Hardin briefly considered retiring from his life of crime and starting a normal life with Jane. While recuperating, he turned himself and his guns in to the sheriff of Cherokee County, Texas, and asked to be charged for his past crimes. Upon hearing how many murder charges he faced, however, he changed his mind. A gang member smuggled him a hacksaw, and he cut through the bars on the jail window to escape.

But it was the 1874 murder of Deputy Sheriff Charles Webb that sent Hardin from Texas and into hiding. He went to meet Jane, whom he had already sent into hiding with their daughter, Mollie, at the home of relatives named Swain in New Orleans. The family left New Orleans using the name "Swain" and headed to Florida.

The pressure to remain hidden grew stronger when the Texas legislature passed a resolution in January 1875 offering "a reward of four thousand

John Wesley Hardin. *Wikimedia Commons.*

dollars for the apprehension and delivery of the body of the notorious murderer, John Wesley Hardin."

While in Jacksonville, Florida, Wes met Gus Kennedy, described by Hardin as a city policeman, and he accompanied the family for the next year.

In August 1875, Hardin's only son, John Wesley Jr., was born. The next summer Hardin, worried Pinkertons were on his trail, sent Jane and the two children to Eufaula, Alabama, while he and Kennedy planned to escape to Mexico. Jane and the children soon ended up with relatives in Pollard. They likely stayed with one of two men: Jane's uncle, Neill McMillan, who was a grocer and deputy sheriff, or Neill's father, Malcolm, the sheriff of Escambia County, Alabama. At times, Hardin was joined by his brother-in-law Brown Bowen, who had been on the lam since murdering Tom Halderman in December 1872. Brown was arrested at the time, but Hardin and his gang helped him escape. Eventually he would join Hardin and his sister in Alabama.

In 1875, Pollard was a town of about six hundred residents. After being burned and occupied by Union troops in March 1865, Pollard had recovered sufficiently in the ensuing years to be home to about a dozen businesses, including saloons, groceries, hotels and a blacksmith.

Unable to reach Mexico, Wes and Kennedy returned to Alabama and in November 1876 traveled to Mobile to gamble.

While there, Hardin, Kennedy and several others got into an argument with a group of men over a card game. Harden claimed in his autobiography that he and Kennedy were arrested after a "running gun battle" in which two Mobile police officers were killed. Newspaper accounts, however, tell another story. No reports mention the death of officers, but one mentions that a local police officer was shot in the arm while he and another officer tried to evict three drunk and disorderly men from a house. The officer's wound was not fatal, and two of the men were arrested while a third got away, the newspaper reported. Those two men were thought to be Hardin and Kennedy.

Their case was heard in Mobile Mayor's Court. Hardin claimed in his autobiography that he paid a $2,500 bribe for his release and that the judge told him "they would leave the city by the first train."

A story in the *Mobile Daily Register* on November 12, 1876, headlined "A Brace of Swindlers" stated:

> *The two sports, Swain and Gus Kennedy, who were arrested several days ago and tried up the charge of malicious mischief, etc., and who were ordered to leave the city, left behind them, as a legacy to the police force, a pack of their swindling cards, which are so marked that they could tell, from their backs, what the faces of the cards were. With these cards they have been swindling unsuspecting players. It is well they were "kicked out of town."*

In 1877, the third and last of Hardin's children, Callie, was born. She was later renamed Jane Martina and called "Jennie." At about the same time, Texas authorities hired two detectives to find him.

When Hardin was captured in Florida in August 1877, he blamed Brown Bowen for giving away his location, saying Brown told a detective his whereabouts. In reality, a Dallas detective named Jack Duncan had been living undercover as a hired hand among Jane Hardin's relatives in Gonzales County. Brown, at that time also hiding in Alabama, inadvertently gave Hardin away when he wrote to his father to say Jane sends her love and mentioned they were using the name "Swain."

The two detectives hired by the State of Texas learned Hardin was not in Pollard but that he was expected soon by train. They went to Pensacola Junction, where they arranged with the sheriff to arrest Hardin on the train as he was returning to Alabama on August 23, 1877.

The detectives took Hardin to Montgomery, Alabama, where a judge ordered him to be transferred to Texas on the charge of murdering Charles Webb. The detectives and Hardin took a train to Memphis, stopping for the night in Decatur, Alabama. By this point, Hardin had given up proclaiming he was Swain and signed the hotel register with his real name.

The men eventually arrived in Austin, Texas, where Hardin was placed in the same jail as Brown Bowen. Brown had been captured in September 1877 and sentenced to die by hanging for the murder of Thomas Halderman. Brown claimed Hardin had killed Halderman, a former member of the gang.

According to many accounts, members of the Bowen family begged Hardin to take the blame for the murder of Tom Halderman. He refused, maintaining his innocence. Jane Bowen Hardin stood by her husband and, as a consequence, became estranged from her father.

A report in the *Gonzalez Inquirer* on May 18, 1878, described Brown's hanging:

It was estimated 4,000 people arrived as to [a] feast to witness the human suffering and shedding of human blood for the hanging of Brown Bowen. The gallows were erected between the jail and the jailer's house so that the prisoner stepped from the head of the stairs onto the platform. The gallows was 17 feet, 6 inches from the top beam to the ground. The platform was 10 feet, 6 inches from the ground. The fall was 7 feet. The trap door was sprung by touching a lever whereupon the door fell to the ground.

About 2:00 p.m., Mr. Bowen was led to the scaffold. Rev. E.Y. Scales read his final statement "blaming his troubles on keeping bad company and proclaiming his innocense [sic] of the murder of Thomas Holderman [sic]."

He claimed that J.W. Hardin, with whom he went to town, killed Holderman [sic] because he thought he was a spy for J. Tomlinson, J. Helms and W.W. Davis. Bowen claimed Hardin and Gip Clements went into the store and started drinking. "Hardin told me he was going to show me how to kill a man. I begged him not to as he (Holderman [sic]) was harmless and my friend. Hardin went to Mr. Holderman [sic] and told him that I killed his son." Bowen prayed with Rev. Seale, the noose around his neck. While Mr. Bass was preparing the spring door, Bowen muttered, "O Lord receive my spirit." The door sprung open and Bowen fell a full 7 feet. In about 6 minutes, he was dead. Bowen was a native of Florida.

Wes was transferred from Austin to Comanche County, where he was convicted in September 1877 for the murder of Deputy Sheriff Charles Webb in 1874. He was sentenced to fifteen years.

After an appeal failed, Hardin was sent to the prison in Huntsville, Texas, on October 5, 1878. He was released from prison in 1894. While in prison, Hardin had studied law, so he emerged with a plan to start a law practice. But he would do so without his beloved, Jane, who had died in 1892.

In 1895, less than a year after his release, Hardin was playing cards in Acme Saloon in El Paso when Constable John Selman Sr. arrived. The *Gonzales Inquirer* reported on Thursday, August 22, 1895:

John Wesley Hardin, the noted Texas desperado, is no more. He was shot and instantly killed to-night about 11:30 o'clock in the Acme saloon by

Above: Grave site of John Wesley Hardin. *Wikimedia Commons*.

Left: A historical marker in Texas describes the crimes of John Wesley Hardin. *Texas State Historical Survey Committee*.

Constable John Sellman. Hardin threatened Sellman's life several times during the evening but on meeting, Sellman was too quick for him.

Sellman, who is very cool and deliberate, but at the same time very quick, has killed a number of bad men and Hardin reckoned without his host when he ran up against him. Hardin fell dead with his boots on before he could get a shot at Sellman...

Wes Hardin, as he was familiarly known over Southwest Texas, was especially the most noted of the living Texas desperadoes. Hardin's early career was spent in DeWitt county, and he was a terror in that section in the '70s, or until he was sent to the penitentiary....

Hardin was the son of a Methodist preacher, and was born in Trinity county being 45 years of age at the time of his death. He was sent to the penitentiary from Lampasas county in 1876 for the killing of the sheriff of Comanche county, who was attempting to arrest him.

CHAPTER 15

AARON BURR

TRIED AS A TRAITOR

In the early days of the United States, a man named Aaron Burr became a hero and went on to become the nation's vice president. But Burr is now more remembered for his transgressions than the service to his country. History records Aaron Burr as the man who killed Alexander Hamilton in a duel and then allegedly plotted to split the Americas by forming an army to forcefully take over Spanish-held territories in America, a plan that would eventually bring him to Alabama.

Aaron Burr was born on February 6, 1756, to Aaron Burr Sr. and Esther Burr in Newark, New Jersey. Aaron Sr. became ill and died in 1757, followed by Esther in 1758, leaving the children orphaned. Aaron and his elder sister briefly went to live with William Shippen and his family until Timothy Edwards adopted the children shortly before marrying his longtime love, Rhoda Ogden, and moving to Elizabeth, New Jersey. In Elizabeth, Aaron Burr became fast friends with Rhoda's two brothers, Aaron and Matthias Ogden, and their neighbor Jonathon Dayton. The friendship would last their entire lives.

Burr was admitted to the College of New Jersey, which later became Princeton University, at the age of thirteen. He obtained his bachelor of arts degree in 1772 after only three years of schooling. He studied theology for the next three years before deciding to change his course of study to law. These studies were cut short when he joined the Continental army in 1775.

During the Revolutionary War, Burr served with distinction. He served as aide-de-camp to General Richard Montgomery in the Battle of Quebec.

Aaron Burr. *Wikimedia Commons.*

Serving under General Putnam in Harlem, Burr helped to save an entire brigade that had been cornered by the British in Manhattan. His actions would make him a hero, although he never received an official commendation.

In 1777, while serving as a lieutenant colonel under Colonel William Malcolm, Burr and his men fought off numerous nighttime British raids in the New Jersey area before making camp in Valley Forge, where he was given a small contingent of soldiers and tasked with guarding the approach to the main army's camp. While there, he stopped an attempted mutiny by some soldiers of the Continental army who were distressed with the harsh winter conditions.

During the Battle of Monmouth on June 27, 1778, Burr collapsed on the battlefield with heat stroke, and even though he recovered, a dramatic decline in his health would cause him to resign his commission with the army in 1779. He returned to his study of law while continuing to perform the occasional intelligence mission for General George Washington.

Even performing these secret missions, Burr was able to continue his studies and was accepted to the New York Bar in 1782 before opening a small legal practice. In 1782, Burr married Theodosia Bartow Prevost. The couple would have one daughter named Theodosia. The couple was married for twelve years before Mrs. Burr died of stomach cancer in 1794.

Burr decided to get involved in politics and went on to have a successful political career. He was twice elected to the New York State Assembly, appointed New York State attorney general, elected a senator from the state of New York and, in his most successful political campaign, was elected as the third vice president of the United States during Thomas Jefferson's first term as president.

Knowing he would not be on the 1804 presidential ballot with Jefferson, Burr decided to run for the position of governor of New York, but he lost the election to Morgan Lewis. Burr blamed this loss on a smear campaign that was headed by then governor George Clinton and supported by Alexander Hamilton. This seems to be the beginning of a bitter rivalry between Burr and Hamilton that continued to escalate during Burr's final year as vice president.

The culmination of their feud came in July 1804, when Burr challenged Hamilton to personal combat under the code duello, which contained the formalized rules of dueling. Dueling had been outlawed in both New York and New Jersey by this time, but since the punishment in New Jersey was less harsh, the two men opted to have their duel outside Weehawken on July 11, 1804.

The two men met at the prearranged location, which had been a common dueling spot, with Alexander Hamilton bringing the guns for the duel. Hamilton would be mortally wounded in the exact same spot where his son had been killed in a previous duel while using the same pistol. The duel was the culmination of a relationship between Hamilton and Burr with many odd twists, including the fact that Hamilton was one of the men whom Burr helped save during the British landing in Manhattan. Because of Hamilton's popularity, the duel would also mark the end of Burr's political career.

Burr was charged with various crimes, including murder in both New York and New Jersey, but because he was the sitting vice president, he was never tried in either jurisdiction, and eventually the charges were dropped. Immediately following the duel, Burr left New York to visit his daughter in South Carolina and then returned to Washington to finish his term as vice president, which he did with little fanfare.

Once Burr left office at the end of his term in 1805, he traveled west. His journey took him through the Ohio River Valley and into the lands obtained during the Louisiana Purchase. It was during this journey that Burr began hatching a plan to form an army and invade the Spanish territories in America after he grew convinced that the Spanish were planning the same thing.

To this end, Burr returned east and began recruiting men to his cause from Pennsylvania and Virginia. He garnered a small force of about one hundred farmers and headed west once again, still attempting to gain support for his idea of creating a colony of men who could quickly rise up against the Spanish in the event of a declaration of war. One of the largest supporters to his cause was none other than Andrew Jackson from Nashville, Tennessee.

Burr had leased forty thousand acres of land along the Ouachita River in what is now Louisiana from the Spanish government, and it was his plan to settle the area with this newly acquired army. Two other important contacts for his plan were General James Wilkinson, who was in charge of the U.S. Army detachment in New Orleans and governor of the Louisiana Territory, and Harman Blennerhassett, who offered his own private island for the training and outfitting of Burr's men.

As Wilkinson pondered the alliance, he determined that he could better serve his own purposes by turning Burr over to the president and the nearby Spanish. Hearing of Burr's plans, President Jefferson declared him a traitor and issued an order for his arrest. Burr was stunned at this turn of events, which he learned from reading a newspaper. Burr was now a wanted man, which meant that he would soon have U.S. government agents on his trail.

On more than one occasion, Burr turned himself in to federal officials, but when he was presented to local judges, they determined that there was no evidence to show Burr had done anything wrong and released him. The fact that local judges released Burr did nothing to keep President Jefferson's warrant from haunting him and causing the former vice president to live the life of a fugitive.

After he was released from his last court hearing in Frankfort, Kentucky, on December 6, 1806, Burr gathered men and boats and took the Cumberland River into Tennessee, where he sought the help of an old friend. Andrew Jackson was glad to assist Burr and helped him to get deep into the Mississippi Territory in what is now the state of Alabama. Burr made a stop in the town that would later be known as Huntsville, Alabama, before continuing farther south toward Spanish-controlled Florida.

On the night of February 18, 1807, two unknown riders were discovered by Nicholas Perkins near the community of Wakefield in Washington County in the Mississippi Territory, an area that would become the Alabama Territory within a decade and then the state of Alabama. The riders stopped and asked Perkins for directions to the nearby home of Major John Hinson. Perkins gave the travelers directions but informed them that the major was not home. The men thanked him and set off for Hinson's home. Perkins was immediately suspicious of the men and, fearing they may be robbers, informed Sheriff Theodore Brightwell of the situation, convincing him to ride to Hinson's home to check the welfare of the absent major's family.

Brightwell and Perkins made their way to the Hinson home, where they found the two men inside warming themselves by the fire. The men were Robert Ashley and the fugitive Aaron Burr. Perkins would later say Sheriff Brightwell seemed enamored of Burr, so he said his goodnights and left the house, heading toward nearby Fort Stoddert to inform soldiers of Burr's whereabouts.

At the fort, Perkins caught the ear of Lieutenant Edward Gaines, who set out the next morning with several men in hopes of intercepting Burr. Gaines and his men met Burr, who was being escorted by Sheriff Brightwell, near the Tombigbee River, where the group had stopped to await the arrival of Burr's servants before boarding a barge heading south. Gaines took the former vice president into custody with no problems and escorted him to Fort Stoddert.

Burr was placed under military guard headed by Lieutenant Gaines for the next several weeks. During his time at the fort, Burr was treated exceptionally well, often taking his dinner with the camp commandant and his family. His treatment was understood as befitting his former position, and in turn, he treated his captors with respect. At no time during his confinement did Burr mention his plans or charges.

In early March, Gaines set out to transfer his famous prisoner to the federal government in Washington, D.C. He escorted Burr to the Alabama River and placed him in a boat with an armed guard. The boat went up the

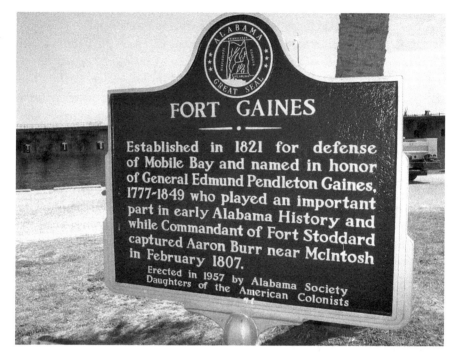

FORT GAINES

Established in 1821 for defense of Mobile Bay and named in honor of General Edmund Pendleton Gaines, 1777-1849 who played an important part in early Alabama History and while Commandant of Fort Stoddard captured Aaron Burr near McIntosh in February 1807.

Erected in 1957 by Alabama Society Daughters of the American Colonists

A marker at Fort Gaines, Alabama, describes Aaron Burr's arrest. *Authors' collection.*

Alabama River into Lake Tensaw. According to legend, women would line the banks and weep at the sight of the former vice president as a prisoner.

At the boatyard in Lake Tensaw, Burr was transferred to the soldiers who would accompany him on the remainder of the long journey north. The soldiers were instructed not to pay attention to what Burr had to say and not to engage him in conversation, lest they be lured into false security by the fugitive's charming personality. Burr was treated with the utmost respect and, for the most part, offered the same to the soldiers. Burr did make one ill-fated escape attempt in Chester, South Carolina, but after its failure, he quietly continued with his captors to await his fate on the charges of treason.

On August 3, 1807, Burr was officially charged with treason in the U.S. Circuit Court in Richmond, Virginia. The lawyers defending Burr were some of the most famous names of the times: Edmund Randolph, John Wickham, Luther Martin and Benjamin Botts. The trial was overseen by John Marshall, chief justice of the United States.

The Constitution requires that treason either be admitted in open court or proved by an overt act witnessed by two people. Since no two witnesses came forward, Burr was acquitted on September 1, despite having the full force of the Jefferson administration's political influence against him. After his acquittal, the prosecution leveled several misdemeanor charges against Burr, but he was also acquitted of these charges.

The legal battles combined with his debt to many creditors left Burr a broken man. After his acquittal, Burr traveled the world, spending a lot of time in England before returning to the United States in the early 1830s, when he became a land speculator. He married for a second time to a wealthy widow named Eliza Jumel. This marriage was short-lived, and she left Burr after only four months of marriage, filing for divorce.

Burr suffered a stroke in 1834 that left him an invalid and in the care of people at a boardinghouse in the village of Port Richmond. Burr died there on September 14, 1836, which oddly enough was the same day that his divorce to Eliza became official.

Burr's body was transported to Princeton, New Jersey, where he was laid to rest near the grave of his father, an unremarkable memorial to a man who was the center of America's first major political scandal.

CHAPTER 16

DAN BOGAN

THE BANDIT WHO DISAPPEARED WITHOUT A TRACE

The name Dan Bogan is not as familiar as those of some frontier gunfighters, perhaps because he often used the aliases Bill Gatlin and Bill McCoy. While his story includes numerous bloody encounters with lawmen, Bogan's life had some unique highlights, including leading a cowboy strike and disappearing without a trace.

No one knows what became of Dan Bogan, who was last heard from in a letter from New Orleans addressed to Tom Hall in Cheyenne, Wyoming. In it, he said he was heading to Argentina.

From all accounts, Dan Bogan's childhood in Alabama was a difficult one. His father, whose name is unknown, died when Dan and his two older brothers were quite young. His mother remarried twice and divorced both men, leaving her with the name D.B. Bogan Oldhous Pierce.

Each marriage produced a daughter, Dan's younger sisters—Emma Oldhous, who was born when Dan was about four years old, and Minnie Pierce, born when Dan was about seven. Census records show Dan's mother and father were born in Alabama—as were Dan, his sisters and, presumably, his elder brothers—but no county is listed.

After his mother's second divorce, she moved with Dan and his siblings to Hamilton County, Texas. It was there that Dan first witnessed violence. His older brothers were caught stealing horses and became embroiled in a gun battle with law officers. One brother was killed; the other was sent to the penitentiary.

Dan was twenty-one years old when he appeared on his first wanted poster in Texas. The incident occurred on May 2, 1881, when he and his friend Dave Kemp went from saloon to saloon in Hamilton, getting more and more inebriated. Dan was spoiling for a fight and, in one saloon, bet he could "lick any man in town." When no one took him up on his challenge, Kemp, realizing trouble was brewing, dragged Dan outside to their horses in an effort to leave town. Dan would have none of it.

When F.A. "Doll" Smith, a well-known local farmer in his thirties, pulled into town on his wagon, Bogan began taunting the man. Doll, who had no idea who Bogan and his friend were, initially ignored the drunken troublemakers. Then, Bogan pulled his gun and threatened Smith.

Dan Bogan. *Wikimedia Commons.*

Smith jumped from the wagon and wrestled Bogan and was able to take his gun, which would have ended the brawl if Kemp had not come up behind Smith and struck him in the head with his pistol. Smith then turned on Kemp and pointed Bogan's confiscated gun at him but did not fire. Kemp attempted to shoot Smith, but his gun kept misfiring. As Smith's attention was on Kemp, Bogan crept up behind Smith and struck him in the head with a rock. Smith staggered from the blow just as Kemp's gun began working. Smith was hit twice and soon fell to the ground, mortally wounded.

Hearing the gunshots, Sheriff G.N. Gentry ran from his office to find himself facing Kemp's gun. After the gun misfired again, Gentry arrested Bogan and Kemp, who were quickly indicted by a grand jury for murder with malice, a death penalty crime.

They were convicted in June 1881, after the trial had been moved to Gatesville because Doll Smith was so well known in Hamilton. Bogan and Kemp were sentenced to death. As the sentence was pronounced, Bogan grabbed a gun from a careless guard, and he and Kemp jumped from the second-floor window of the courthouse. Kemp broke a leg and was soon recaptured. Bogan jumped onto a horse and fled to freedom in what would be the first of many escapes. After an appeal, Kemp was retried and sentenced to twenty-five years.

For the next two decades, Bogan would be a regular on most wanted lists for such callous acts as killing a dance hall proprietor while shooting up a Texas town to celebrate the end of a workweek. Bogan, who was described as five feet, ten inches tall and weighing about 175 pounds with dark eyes and brown hair, took work as a drover in the Texas Panhandle, calling himself Bill Gatlin.

The cowboys, unhappy with their twenty-five-dollar-per-week pay, began organizing a strike. In April 1883, the cowboys attempted a strike, demanding pay to be increased to fifty dollars per week for cowhands and seventy-five dollars per week for crew bosses. The strike failed, and Bogan, as ringleader, was blacklisted by ranchers throughout the panhandle.

Unable to find legal work as a cowboy, Bogan teamed up with rustlers and began changing brands on cattle to steal them. Tiring of the thefts, ranch owners commissioned Pat Garrett—the former sheriff of Lincoln County, New Mexico, credited with breaking up Billy the Kid's gang—to stop the rustlers.

In the fall of 1884, a grand jury handed down 159 indictments against rustlers, and Garrett and his home guard set out to arrest those who had been charged, including the man who called himself Bill Gatlin.

With Garrett on their trails, most of the rustlers left the territory, all but Bogan, Wade Woods and Charlie Thompson, who said they refused to be driven out.

It took until February 1885 for Garrett and the home guard to track the men to a house in Tascosa, Texas. They hollered for the men to surrender. Thompson said Woods was not in the house, but he agreed to come out with his hands up. Bogan refused until the local sheriff went inside and assured Bogan that he would have protection from a lynch mob.

After his surrender, Bogan and Thompson were taken to the local jail, a small adobe building with iron bars on the windows. One of their confederates soon slipped them a file, and Dan Bogan once again escaped justice.

Bogan was next heard from using the name Bill McCoy near Jackson Hole, Wyoming, where he was a hand at Vorhees Ranch moonlighting as a horse thief. He would soon find himself on the wrong side of the law once again.

In about 1886, Bill Calkin, the editor of a newspaper in Lusk, Wyoming, reported "Bill McCoy" was possibly a man wanted in Texas. An angry Bogan and his friend Sterling Balou went looking for Calkin to challenge him to fight. They found him at a local saloon, where Bogan drew his gun but was soon in a standoff with locals, who also drew their weapons. When local Constable Charles S. Gunn, a former Texas Ranger with a reputation as a tough lawman, wandered into the fray with his own pistol drawn, Dan Bogan fled.

After Bogan went on another wild run through town a few days later, Gunn gave the cowboy a warning: Don't let it happen again—or else. Bogan was humiliated at being repeatedly reprimanded by Gunn but, by most accounts, also feared the lawman. After one more reprimand, Bogan could take no more embarrassment. On January 15, 1887, Bogan shot Gunn in the stomach, and as Gunn lay on the floor of the Jim Waters Saloon, Bogan shot him again in the head.

He rode off on a stolen horse with Deputy Marshal John Owens on his heels. Owens shot Bogan in the shoulder, knocked him from his saddle and imprisoned him in a backroom of the saloon. The next day, during a blizzard, the wily Bogan escaped, but he didn't get far. When his wound got infected, he was forced to surrender.

Townspeople were unwilling to forgive the fact that Bogan brutally murdered their beloved constable and soon formed a lynch mob to meet Owens returning to town with Bogan. Owens had to promise the crowd that Bogan would get justice to calm its ire. The next day, Owens transported Bogan to a secure jail in Cheyenne, Wyoming, where the outlaw went on trial. The *Cheyenne Daily Leader* reported, "Without provocation or pity he ruthlessly murdered a man far superior to himself in every way—and has murdered two other men."

After Bogan was convicted of murder and the judge pronounced he was to be hanged by the neck until he was "dead, dead, dead," the newspaper reported that Bogan "appeared completely unconcerned."

Bogan may have seemed unconcerned as he heard the death sentence, but he was likely merely planning. He still had cowboy friends, and convicted murdered Tom Nicholls, going by the name Tom Hall, paid a professional safecracker to commit a minor crime and get captured so he could help Bogan break out from the inside. He and Bogan sawed through the bars and escaped on October 4, 1887, along with horse thieves Charles H. LeRoy and Bill Steary. Tom Hall was waiting with a saddled horse, and the two rode out of Cheyenne.

Quickly, officials posted a $1,000 reward for Bogan, dead or alive. The *Cheyenne Daily Leader* reported, "Dan Bogan, alias Wm. McCoy, is a Texas desperado and a fugitive from that state…[He] is a reckless and blood thirsty

An illustration of Dan Bogan from a wanted poster. *Public domain.*

character and the assertion is ventured he will not be taken alive."

One of the largest manhunts in Wyoming was soon underway, and when Bogan could not be flushed out, the famed Pinkerton's National Detective Agency was called and Charlie Siringo assigned to the case.

Siringo always stayed one step behind Bogan, but he eventually heard that Bogan had said he was tired of living on the lam and was headed to New Orleans to take a ship to South America. At one point, Siringo heard Bogan was traveling with a twelve-year-old boy who, growing attached to the outlaw, begged to accompany him to South America. Bogan refused, fearing the boy would slow him down and lead to his capture, and told him if he tried to follow him he would kill him. Bogan rode away, and the boy followed, only to have his horse return the next day, its saddle covered in dried blood.

Bogan did make it to New Orleans, where he sent a letter to Tom Hall in Cheyenne saying he was headed to Argentina. After that, legend takes over.

Newspapers often reported Bogan's demise. The *Laramie Sentinel* wrote in 1889 that Bogan had been killed in Mexico; another newspaper reported he'd died in 1907 from a broken neck after his horse bucked him.

But in 1919, when Siringo published a memoir, *A Lone Star Cowboy*, he said he thought Bogan was still alive. He wrote that he thought Bogan had returned to the States under another assumed name, married and raised a family in New Mexico. Siringo wrote, "The chances are Bill Gatlin, alias Bill McCoy, would sweat blood did he know that I knew his present name and address, for the hangman's noose would stare him in the face. If he really did kill that boy, he should be hanged more than once."

CHAPTER 17

BUSHWHACKER MILUS JOHNSTON

OUTLAW TO THE UNION, HERO TO THE SOUTH

Outlaws come in many forms, and oftentimes, the line that separates outlaw from upstanding citizen is blurred. This has never been more apparent than during the American Civil War, when outlaws on both sides of the Mason-Dixon line were more often than not called bushwhackers. In the context of war, acts committed by bushwhackers were considered crimes by the opposing side. It is also fair to note that sometimes these bushwhackers simply took up arms to protect their communities.

Such is the case with one north Alabama minister who laid down his Bible to take up arms against Union forces he felt were harassing his flock. The pastor became so prolific in his abilities that he actually became known as Milus "Bushwhacker" Johnston, a name that struck fear in many a Union soldier occupying northern Alabama.

Milus Johnston. *Madison County Historical Society.*

Milus Eddings Johnston was born on July 26, 1823, to Oliver Campbell Johnston and Hannah Hall Buckley Johnston in Wilson County near Lebanon, Tennessee. He had a strict upbringing and was well educated, graduating from the Brush Creek Law School in Smith County, Tennessee, at the age of sixteen. Later that year, he became "born again" in the Methodist Church, and he began ministerial studies. In 1840, he was appointed as a Methodist preacher in the Smith Forks and Carthage areas.

In 1843, Johnston married Susan Anna Ray, and the couple would have five children, three sons and two daughters, before Susan's death in 1853.

After Susan's death, Milus continued to preach while also raising his children and battling increasingly poor health. He would move his family to Madison County, Alabama, after hearing the area around Monte Sano Mountain had healing properties. In Alabama, Johnston met local widow Mary Hamer Findley and again fell in love. The two courted and then married on October 21, 1859. Johnston worked as a Methodist circuit preacher, serving the Vienna, Larkinsville and Madison circuits in Alabama and the Fayetteville, Tennessee circuit.

Before the beginning of the Civil War, Johnston was a Unionist who did not want the country to split. Even though many residents in the Huntsville and Madison County area did not support the Union, they, too, were against dividing the country. The onset of the Civil War made those objections moot. Johnston, like so many others, took this turn of events in stride and decided to support his home state.

While performing ministerial duties in Fayetteville in 1862, he ran afoul of the Union army, which had moved into the areas around Fayetteville after the Battle of Shiloh. On multiple occasions, Johnston tried to reach the churches on his circuit, only to be rebuffed by the Union military. Johnston was eventually threatened with arrest, so he returned home to Madison County, burning with a desire to fight to protect his followers.

At the same time, Lemuel Mead of Jackson County, Alabama, had been recommissioned from the Fiftieth Alabama Infantry to that of cavalry captain. He was asked to recruit a company of "partisan rangers" to operate behind the enemy lines in the north Alabama and southern Tennessee theaters.

The formation of this group was the perfect situation for Johnston, who could remain near his home and perform his ministerial duties while fighting to protect the rights of parishioners to worship. He joined the rangers, and the unit quickly and quietly made a name for itself. Through 1862, guerrilla fighters in Paint Rock, Alabama, continually harassed Union troops from the Third Ohio under Colonel John Beatty. The Union forces suffered nine casualties from a sniper attack, and Beatty threatened to burn a house and hang a man for each of his soldiers killed. He then set the town ablaze and took three civilian prisoners. Reports say that the commander of the army in Huntsville, General Ormsby Mitchel, was pleased with Beatty's actions.

The Union's occupation of Huntsville was difficult and often bloody. The arriving Union forces had expected to find a strongly pro-Union population in northern Alabama; instead, General Mitchel's force found a region deeply divided among Unionist and Confederate, slave and free, black and white. The counties south of the Tennessee River were notoriously Unionist, populated with farmers who had no interest in struggles to preserve slavery. In the counties along the Tennessee River, however, farmers joined with large slaveholders in the river bottoms and fertile plains that were ideal for cotton planting. Unionists and secessionists in northern Alabama were neighbors, business partners and kin. Geography and custom tied the region economically to Tennessee to the north.

Even in this politically charged environment, pro-Confederate sentiment grew, and guerrilla attacks increased and were met with escalating reprisals. General Mitchel found it difficult enough to maintain order in his widely spread forces, and the guerrilla attacks exacerbated a volatile situation. He begged his commanders for more troops, particularly cavalry. He wired to Washington that "armed citizens fire into the trains, cut the telegraph wires, attack the guards of bridges, cut off and destroy my couriers, while guerrilla bands of cavalry attack whenever there is the slightest chance of success." But the general never received his reinforcements, and the cycle of violence in the area continued.

In September 1862, the Union army pulled out of the area, leaving Mead and his forces with limited activities to pursue. It also gave respite to the citizens who had been living in the middle of the guerrilla violence and Union retaliation. This period of decreased activity provided time for Mead's forces to train and develop other skills that the soldiers would need when the Union army returned in 1863.

In January 1864, Mead was authorized to expand his company into a cavalry battalion. Mead's men, including Johnston, who was now a captain, constantly harassed the Union invaders, attacked the railroad, captured wagon trains, broke up forage parties and forced the Union army to keep several regiments dedicated to defending against them.

In November and December 1864, the battalion assisted the Fourth Alabama Cavalry in support of General John Bell Hood's Nashville

Above: Union troops mustered around the Madison County courthouse square during the 1862 occupation of Huntsville. *Madison County Historical Society.*

Left: Milus Johnston. *Madison County Historical Society.*

campaign, but this was not the unit's most famous operation. That came on New Year's Eve 1864. The still unnamed rangers conducted a raid on the Union detachment at Paint Rock Bridge. The small Confederate force captured roughly fifty soldiers of the Eighteenth Wisconsin Infantry along with a Union howitzer, a great accomplishment for the small group. The capture earned it the notice of the Confederate brass.

In March 1865, Mead received an appointment to colonel and was authorized to re-form his men into an official regiment, which became known as the Twenty-fifth Alabama Cavalry and the Twenty-seventh Tennessee Cavalry. Captain Johnston, who by now had earned the nickname "Bushwhacker," was named a lieutenant colonel and placed in command of the Twenty-fifth Alabama. But these units would be short-lived.

With the surrender of Lee's forces at Appomattox, Virginia, and the end of the Confederacy looming, Colonel Johnston was forced to surrender his men in Huntsville on May 11, 1865. Colonel Mead and his Twenty-seventh Tennessee held out for a few more weeks encamped on Brindlee Mountain, but they also disbanded by the end of May 1865.

With the war over, Milus Eddings Johnston returned to his home in New Hope, where he resumed his life of dedication to the ministry. He preached for the next thirty years before retiring in 1895 as his hearing began to fail. Later in life, Johnston hesitated to talk about his experiences during the war, preferring instead to talk about the ministry. Johnston returned to Tennessee, where he peacefully passed away on October 8, 1915, at the age of ninety-two.

CHAPTER 18

AYE! THERE BE PIRATE TALES IN ALABAMA

Although Alabama's coastline is relatively short—less than sixty miles—there have been some pirate tales associated with it. Some are merely legend. A few pirates—like Michel de Grammont, François le Sage and Du Chesne—cruised along Alabama's coastline once or twice and often only when wind forced them north while sailing to or from Mexico. But those who did make landfall had an impact on the state's history.

Attack on Dauphin Island

In 1710, privateers, or lawfully commissioned pirates, invaded the small, isolated island off Alabama's Gulf Coast. Dauphin Island, then a colony of France called Massacre Island, had only about twenty structures at the time, and its inhabitants were dependent on France for food and supplies. It was also a wild and lawless place, and its people refused to work the soil to grow crops, preferring to drink and brawl late into the nights. Their main sources of food were fishing and oyster harvesting.

The privateer ship, commissioned by the governor of Jamaica, arrived on the island on September 9, 1710. It was a brigantine, a two-masted vessel armed with cannon.

The privateers took eight or nine thousand deerskins, fifteen thousand raccoon skins, some other pelts, seventy-one barrels of flour and some naval stores over three days. The men tortured residents to get them to tell if there were hidden valuables and burned most of the buildings before leaving the island.

According to legend, when the settlers saw the approaching ships, they took action to hide any valuables, including a bejeweled gold cross.

While there is no evidence the colonists would have had access to such finery, lore says the island's Catholic church had the cross mounted at its top and that fishermen used it as a landmark. When privateers approached, the islanders reportedly dropped the cross in a well to prevent its being stolen, and it was never recovered.

Although the attack on Dauphin Island was the only verified invasion by sea rovers on Alabama's coast, many stories mention various pirates' connections to the state.

Here is a look at some pirates whose history, however slightly, mingles with Alabama's.

Laurens de Graff

Laurens de Graff, a seventeenth-century buccaneer, was a Dutchman who served as a Spanish gunner aboard pirate-hunting ships before he was captured by pirates and soon joined them. De Graff also fought in the only confirmed duel between two pirate captains. He won, and the other captain later died from his wounds. De Graff was pardoned for the duel, however, and later became a French citizen and naval officer.

Laurens Cornelis Boudewijn de Graff was born circa 1653 and died on May 24, 1704. He also went by the names Laurencillo or El Griffe in Spanish, Sieur de Baldran in French and Gesel van de West, meaning Scourge of the West, in Dutch. De Graff—described by Henry Morgan, the governor of Jamaica, as "mischievous"—looked nothing like fictional pirates who are dark, swarthy and bearded. De Graff was tall and blond and wore a handlebar mustache. He was considered quite handsome. He was a bit of a rock star of his time, often accompanied by crowds and fiddlers when he went ashore.

De Graff visited Mobile Bay but not to attack or plunder. In 1698, he piloted a ship in Pierre Le Moyne d'Iberville's expedition to the Gulf Coast. Although De Graff was last known to be near Louisiana, some people believe he was still on the Gulf Coast when he died in 1704 and could be buried in

Old Mobile or Biloxi, Mississippi. However, most evidence indicates that he returned to Saint-Domingue in 1699.

GASPARILLA

Gasparilla was a legendary Spanish pirate who is said to have raided the Florida coast in the late eighteenth and early nineteenth centuries and buried treasure chests near Mobile in the early nineteenth century.

The legend is likely based on a pirate named José Gaspar, who was born in Spain in 1756 and served in the Spanish navy. Gaspar reportedly kidnapped a young girl for ransom and joined the navy rather than be sent to jail. Other stories say he mutinied while aboard a ship and soon became a pirate.

His other legendary exploits credit him with being a member of the court of King Charles III, but when a jilted lover accused him of theft (some versions say he was accused of taking the crown jewels), he commandeered a ship and turned pirate to escape arrest, roaming the Gulf Coast from 1783 to 1821.

Gaspar reportedly buried several chests of pirate loot at various locations in Mobile Bay.

JEAN LAFITTE

For decades, tales have circulated that notorious pirate Jean Lafitte spent time in the coastal Alabama towns of Bayou La Batre and Coden and may have buried treasure there. Some of the legends claim Lafitte himself may have died here and is buried in Alabama soil.

Historians, however, say the only recorded visit by Lafitte to Alabama was in 1815 to settle a legal dispute in Mobile over the percentage of proceeds to be paid to him for sale of a vessel named *Adventurer*.

Jean Lafitte was born circa 1778, either in France or Saint-Domingue, which was a French colony. He would eventually become known as both pirate and hero, being called at varying times the "Corsair," the "King of Barataria," "Terror of the Gulf," "Hero of the Battle of New Orleans" and the "Buccaneer." Lafitte reportedly hated the label "pirate," preferring "privateer." As evidence to support Lafitte's dueling persona, U.S. presidents

Drawing of Jean Lafitte. *Wikimedia Commons.*

This portrait is believed to be of Jean Lafitte. *Wikimedia Commons.*

at varying times condemned him for his crimes and then exonerated him only to condemn him again. Although he swore no allegiance to his country of birth, Lafitte is said to have never attacked an American ship out of respect for the fledgling nation's Constitution and ideals.

He was considered charming and elegant and was fluent in four languages: English, French, Italian and Spanish. Jean and his brother Pierre Lafitte led a smuggling and slave-trafficking operation by 1805, using a warehouse in New Orleans to house stolen goods. The operation was moved in 1807 to the three islands of Barataria Bay, Louisiana, where it grew into a successful business.

Some records indicate the brothers had a fleet of fifty ships and as many as one thousand men based in Barataria Bay and plundered ships along the Gulf Coast for art, furniture, clothing, silks, dinnerware, wines, medicines and slaves. Lafitte was based on Barataria's Grand Terre Island, which he populated with privateers and pirates, ship's carpenters, cooks, sail makers and navigators.

The fleet was captured in 1814 when Americans invaded the island. Jean Lafitte agreed to help General Andrew Jackson defend New Orleans against the British in 1815 in exchange for a pardon on smuggling and piracy charges. The brothers later acted as spies for the Spanish during the Mexican War of Independence.

Eventually, the Lafittes would form a pirate colony called Campeche on Galveston Island, Texas. Jean reportedly married Madeline Regaud in about 1820 in Galveston. They had one son, Jean Pierre Lafitte, who would die in 1832.

According to published accounts, including one in a Colombian newspaper, Lafitte died in 1823 from wounds received battling Spanish privateers in the Gulf of Honduras. He most likely would have been buried at sea.

Although pirates with large operations at the time used banks, legends persist in Alabama that Jean Lafitte buried $80,000 in gold coins on a beach in Bayou La Batre.

BIBLIOGRAPHY

(Note: These sources are in addition to some of the periodicals with direct attributions in each chapter.)

Agee, George W. *Rube Burrow: King of the Outlaws and His Band of Train Robbers.* Chicago: Henneberry Co., 1890.

Alabama Department of Archives and History.

Alabama Genealogy Trails. "Bibb County Alabama Crime News Items." genealogytrails.com.

Alabama State Archives. Ninth Alabama Infantry record.

American History. USHistory.org.

Autobiography of Albert Parsons. 1887. Recorded by University of Missouri–Kansas City. umkc.edu.

Bernston, Ben. "Railroad Bill." Encyclopedia of Alabama. www. EncyclopediaofAlabama.org.

Bibb County Historical Review.

Borelli, Stephen. *How about That! The Life of Mel Allen.* Champaign, IL: Sports Publishing LLC, 2005.

Bridgeport Morning News, October 28, 1889.

Cheyenne Daily Leader, October 5, 1887. From Nolan, Frederick W. *Tascosa: Its Life and Gaudy Times.* Lubbock: Texas Tech University Press, 2007.

Chicago History Museum. ChicagoHistory.org.

Chicago Tribute Markers of Distinction. ChicagoTribute.org.

Copeland Gang. ThePastWhispers.com/Copeland_Gang, extracted from Perry County, Mississippi Works Progress Administration Files.

Cronan, J. Michael. "Trial of the Century! The Acquittal of Frank James." *Missouri Historical Review* 91, no. 2 (January 1997).

Dale County, Alabama Archives.

DauphinIslandHistory.org.

DeArment, Robert K. *Deadly Dozen: Twelve Forgotten Gunfighters of the Old West.* Vol. 1. Norman: University of Oklahoma Press, 2003.

ehistory by Ohio State University. ehistory.osu.edu.

1880 census, Hamilton County, Texas.

1850 census, Mobile County, Alabama.

Ellison, Regina Hines. "Americus." Published on co.jackson.ms.us, 1988.

Ellison, Rhoda Coleman. *Bibb County: The First One Hundred Years.* Tuscaloosa: University of Alabama Press, n.d.

———. "Outlaws, Cat's-Paws, and Spotters." *Alabama Heritage* no. 8 (Spring 1988).

Encyclopedia of Alabama. "Choctaw County." www.EncyclopediaofAlabama.org.

Escambia County, Alabama Historical Society.

Evening Bulletin, Maysville, Kentucky.

Explore Southern History. "The Battle of Newton." ExploreSouthernHistory.com.

FindAGrave.com.

Florence Times, Alabama, March 4, 1893.

Fort Worth Daily Gazette, December 12, 1886.

Gay, Ann Harwell, author of *The Perverse Prophet and Choctaw County's Sims War*, 1990. Telephone interview, February 2014.

Genealogytrails.com. "Choctaw County Crime News." Alabama Genealogy Trails. "Choctaw County Alabama Crime News Items." genealogytrails.com

Geringer, Joseph. "Jean Lafitte: Gentleman Pirate of New Orleans." crimelibrary.com.

Hall, Jim. Interview with the authors. September 2013.

Hamilton Free Press, Marion County, Alabama, January 25, 1894.

Hardin, John Wesley. *The Life of John Wesley Hardin: As Written by Himself.* Seguin, TX: Smith & Moore, 1896.

Historical Marker Database. hmdb.org.

History.com.

History Matters. American Social History Project/Center for Media and Learning. historymatters.gmu.edu.

Illinois Labor History Society. IllinoisLaborHistory.org.

Johnston, Milus E., and Charles S. Rice. *The Sword of Bushwhacker Johnston: Including a Complete Roster of Mead's Battalion, Confederate Cavalry.* Huntsville, AL: Flint River Press, 1992.

Kennedy, Jo Myrtle. *Dauphin Island, French Possession, 1699–1763.* Huntsville, AL: Strode Publishers, 1980.

Lauderdale County, Alabama Archives.

Lewis Thornton Powell web page. lewisthorntonpowell.com.

Little, Benerson, former Navy SEAL and author of five books on pirates. Interview.

Los Angeles Herald 37, no. 68, December 27, 1891.

Madison County, Alabama Historical Archives.

Milwaukee Journal, December 29, 1893.

Palladium, Oswego, New York, September 15, 1896.

Perry County, Mississippi Works Progress Administration files.

Pickett, Albert James. *History of Alabama, and Incidentally of Georgia and Mississippi: From the Earliest Period.* Charleston, SC: Walker and James, 1851.

Pittsburgh Press, December 27, 1891.

Pitts, Dr. J.R.S. *Life and Confessions of the Noted Outlaw James Copeland, Executed at Augusta, Perry County, Mississippi.* N.p., 1909.

"Railroad Bill." jayssouth.com, 2007.

Ratliff, John H. "The Simite Extermination." *Alabama Review* 66, no. 4 (October 2013).

Robison, Jim. "Lincoln Conspirator's Skull Laid to Rest." *Orlando Sentinel*, November 13, 1994.

Rogers, William Warren, and Ruth Pruitt. *Alabama's Outlaw Sheriff, Stephen S. Renfroe.* Tuscaloosa: University of Alabama Press, 2005.

San Francisco Call 71, no. 27, December 27, 1891.

Siringo, Charles A. *A Lone Star Cowboy.* Facsimile of 1919 original edition.

Southern Star, Wednesday, April 12, 1899.

Texas State Historical Association. tshaonline.org.

Times-Daily, Florence, Alabama, March 30, 1895.

Times-Picayune, August 9, 1891.

"A Traitor in the Wilderness: The Arrest of Aaron Burr." *Alabama Heritage* 83 (Winter 2007).

Tuscaloosa News, August 5, 1973.

———, May 7, 1980.

200 Years of Jackson County, a timeline at tikitoki.com.

Van Der Veer Hamilton, Virginia. *Alabama: A History.* New York: W.W. Norton and Company, 1984.

The War of the Rebellion: A Compilation of the Official Records of the Union and Confederate Armies. 70 vols. Washington, D.C.: Government Printing Office, 1880–1901. Accessed from the Lauderdale County Historical Archives.

Wilson, Claire M. "Rube Burrow." Encyclopedia of Alabama. www.EncyclopediaofAlabama.org.

Winborne, Lucie. "Two Very Different Men, Part II: The Strange Journey of Lewis Thornton Powell." June 3, 2013. http://lmwinborne.wordpress.com.

Wright, A.J. "A Gunfighter's Southern Vacation." *Quarterly of the National Association and Center for Outlaw and Lawmen* (1982).

Writers Program. *Alabama: A Guide to the Deep South.* Works Progress Administration, state of Alabama, 1941.

ABOUT THE AUTHORS

W il Elrick hails from Guntersville, Alabama, where at an early age he developed a love for both trivia and history. He has spent the last twenty-odd years fine-tuning the art of communication while working in law enforcement, television media, historical research and public speaking. He lives in north Alabama with his two boys and a neurotic German shepherd. Wil one day hopes that Bigfoot is proven real. If you would like to contact Wil, please e-mail him at notquitedead@outlook.com.

K elly Kazek has been a journalist for twenty-eight years, specializing in Alabama history. She is the author of seven previous books, including a collection of humor columns and books on regional history. She has won numerous state and national writing awards. She lives in Madison, Alabama, with her daughter and her trusty side-dog, Lucy. As crazy as it sounds, she is planning to marry her coauthor.

CPSIA information can be obtained
at www.ICGtesting.com
Printed in the USA
BVHW050031090223
658189BV00003B/143